SWEET SUCCESS
HOW NUTRASWEET CREATED
A BILLION DOLLAR BUSINESS

SWEET SUCCESS
HOW NUTRASWEET CREATED A
BILLION DOLLAR BUSINESS

Joseph E. McCann

BUSINESS ONE IRWIN
Homewood, Illinois 60430

This publication is designed to provide accurate and
authoritative information in regard to the subject matter
covered. It is sold with the understanding that neither the
author nor the publisher is engaged in rendering legal, accounting,
or other professional service. If legal advice or other expert
assistance is required, the services of a competent
professional person should be sought.

*From a Declaration of Principles jointly adopted by a Committee
of the American Bar Association and a Committee of Publishers.*

Senior editor: Jeffrey Krames
Project editor: Karen Nelson
Production manager: Carma W. Fazio
Jacket designer: Image House
Compositor: Carlisle Communications, Ltd.
Typeface: 11/13 Century Schoolbook
Printer: The Book Press, Inc.

Library of Congress Cataloging-in-Publication Data

McCann, Joseph E.
    Sweet success : how NutraSweet created a billion dollar business /
Joseph E. McCann.
        p.   cm.
    Includes bibliographical references.
    ISBN 1-55623-268-3
    1. Sweetener industry—United States.   I. Title.
    HD9105.M33   1990
338.4'76645—dc20   90–3305
                                                                    CIP

Printed in the United States of America
1 2 3 4 5 6 7 8 9 0 BP 7 6 5 4 3 2 1 0

To Emory Business School for its unquestioning support, and my family members for their patience

PREFACE

Sweet Success has two major objectives. At its simplest level, it tries to be an entertaining story about one company's success. We need success stories these days, particularly when they are about small companies winning against larger competitors, many of them in foreign countries. In this instance, the story is about possibly the most popular food additive ever created. Aspartame did not simply ride the diet and health food wave, but actually amplified it. The NutraSweet Company is the vanguard of the emerging "high tech" food companies which are changing the very way we relate to food.

The second important objective is to use the NutraSweet story as a vehicle to explore the challenges facing young, technology-intensive companies trying to enter intensely competitive, increasingly global industries. The NutraSweet Company is a model of what it is like to compete in such an industry.

The irony of doing a book like this one is that, with the exception of a few "oldtimers" in NutraSweet, you eventually come to know more about the company's history and current situation than most of its employees. History began, in many of their eyes, in 1982 when NutraSweet was established within G. D. Searle & Co. as a separate profit center with Bob Shapiro at its head. Creation was even more recent if you consider that it began when Searle's NutraSweet Group was combined by Monsanto on January 1, 1986 with Searle's Equal brand business and set up as a separate operating company.

This mental veil is amazing, since aspartame's potential as a sweetener was discovered 17 years earlier by James Schlatter, a bench chemist who (as the story goes) licked his finger while turning a page of a notebook. Dan Searle admits the event was fortuitous, but was also bad science. As is so often the case in lab discoveries, Schlatter had been working on another application for aspartame—in ulcer treatments, Dan recalls. Tasting fingers, however, isn't good lab protocol. Nonetheless, piecing together the story of those ensuing 17 years, as well as what the company has done since, has turned out to be a remarkable odyssey and much more than a study of a new product introduction.

This trip is mapped in the next chapters. The natural break between Chapters 2 and 3 is marked by the entry in 1977 of new leadership within Searle—Donald Rumsfeld as CEO and John Robson as president, both coming out of government careers, and James Denny as chief financial officer coming from The Firestone Tire & Rubber Co. Their entry marked the passage of one more corporate family dynasty. Many of the most critical events occurred with aspartame across this leadership transition, but the entry of Rumsfeld, Robson, and, subsequently, Bob Shapiro in 1979 began a dramatically different regime within Searle. With their entry, Searle moved smoothly from a family-run company to a professionally managed corporation with a uniquely talented team of three former government executives at its helm.

Chapters 2 through 5 explore the early days, including:

- The discovery of aspartame's use, and the risky decision to pursue FDA approval.
- The selection and early relationship with Ajinomoto Company, the giant Japanese food company Searle subsequently negotiated a joint-venture agreement with to produce aspartame.
- The decision to regain some control of aspartame technology, and thus regain independence from Ajinomoto, by secretly "bootstrapping" development of a new process for a key ingredient.
- The agonizing regulatory process that included the FDA's 1974 yanking of the first approval, and subsequent 7-year battle with critics, which so demoralized the company that it even wrote off $21 million in inventory just months before approval was finally given.
- The successful, quiet attempt engineered by John Robson to get aspartame's patent life extended by getting a "one-legged Hopi" amendment passed in the closing hours

of Congress, thus giving NutraSweet the time needed to create a business.

- How NutraSweet muscled and stumbled into markets dominated by food giants like PepsiCo, tilting the balance of the "Cola Wars" in the process.
- The encouraging story of life in the three plants during their start-ups—how American R&D, engineering, and manufacturing were wedded in different ways to create world class production.

All of these streams of events, and more, overlapped. Telling such a complex story becomes a formidable task. It's easy to see why the red and white swirl was adopted for the NutraSweet logo—life was an incredible swirl of events and people during this time! Actually, the swirl better symbolizes the fermentation and blending process which creates aspartame.

Chapter 6 looks at NutraSweet since Monsanto's acquisition. What isn't known until now is that it was NutraSweet's presence that almost ruined the deal for Searle; Monsanto wanted a pharmaceutical company, and NutraSweet was the "ugly duckling" with an unknown future. But the Monsanto-NutraSweet relationship is easily one of the best examples of successful post-acquisition management today. This chapter looks at what was done to make it succeed, and examines NutraSweet's future from the perspective of the options and choices facing it from January 1986 to the present.

The obvious danger in writing a book about a company facing big choices is that you can get surprised about how things turn out by the time you get to print. Ask Tom Peters and Bob Waterman, authors of *In Search of Excellence,* or any number of other "current events" authors about that danger. NutraSweet is an excellent company in many, many ways, but one of this book's goals is to highlight the options and choices, both good and less good, made along the path to the present.

All organizations face critical decision points in their development that become true watershed events capable of fundamentally shaping their futures. Whether an organization's leadership is able to either recognize, and even better, to force those transition points is an excellent question. Do they stumble into them, only to make

sense of what happened afterwards—leadership by post-hoc ratio-
nalization, with idolization of successful outcomes and "poignant"
case studies of those without? Or do they move step-by-step, incre-
mentally probing and poking for a sense of direction as some
researchers like James Brian Quinn have noted?[1] Or is there some-
where within the organization a "grand strategy" guiding and or-
chestrating the decisions and actions of management? With all the
talk nowadays about visionary leadership, these are important
questions, indeed.[2]

The NutraSweet story contains elements of all of these
approaches, to be very honest, but what is so intriguing is to see
how the organization has learned over time. Organizational
learning has occurred, and the learning process is accelerating
even further. In the emerging innovation race, organizations
that fail to learn will simply fail. Period. How has NutraSweet's
organizational learning process worked? That's part of the story
Sweet Success tells.

A second goal is to describe what the company is doing to
prepare itself to create its future. The task is not so much to extol,
but to explain. What are the company's choices, and how does it
go about weighing them? To what degree does the firm's history
and culture, previous decisions, and perceptions of its industry
and self play roles in envisioning and bringing about its future?
These are the questions which *Sweet Success* turns to now.

Searle and NutraSweet's development of aspartame's use as
a sweetener spans more than 20 years, and a major premise of
Sweet Success is that the context for innovation has radically
transformed during this time—the emergence of an entirely new
playing field for technology-intensive companies. NutraSweet's
leadership understands these changes and has responded. Chapter 7 describes the dimensions of these new conditions and their
implications for technology-intensive companies like NutraSweet. This transformation is the result of the complex dynamics between our culture, technology, and (very important for

---

[1]J. B. Quinn, "Managing Innovation: Controlled Chaos," *Harvard Business Review*,
May–June 1985, pp. 73–84.

[2]See, for example, Warren Bennis, *On Becoming a Leader* (Reading, Mass.: Addison-
Wesley Publishing, 1989).

the present situation) our government's attempts at managing the interaction between culture and technology. The results of these interactions among culture, technology, and government are seen in fundamental paradigm shifts from:

Machine Age to Organic Thinking—the blurring of boundaries between industries and groups, coming from the recognition and acceptance of interdependence.

Monolithic to Pluralistic Models—power sharing across organizations, classes of society, and countries.

Competition to Collaboration—you can win by working with friends more easily than going it alone.

Structure to Process—how we do things is just as important as what we do.

Technology Programs to Technology Pulses—the pace of innovation is continuous and is no longer punctuated by "breathing spaces" that allow catching up.

National to Transnational—the unit of analysis for everything is now global.

Short-Term to Long-Term Thinking—the preoccupation with immediate economic rationality is *finally* giving way to institutional level strategy that emphasizes the firm's positioning for a much more distant future.

Much of the conflict and failure of organizations and governments to win at global technological innovation is due to their inability to recognize and accept these shifts. NutraSweet has been able to recognize these sweeping changes, but still struggles like every other firm to navigate the changes they manifest themselves in every day and in many ways.

Chapter 8 is a key chapter. It presents a simple conceptual model called the competitive wedge to help describe and relate several design principles revealed from the NutraSweet story. The notion of "wedge" versus "edge" is more than a play on words. The competitive wedge model argues that it is the unique configuration of the company's products and services, structure and systems, people, and technologies which creates truly sustainable competitive advantage. Each of these components is a competitive edge—a potentially unique basis for competing. However, it is only when these edges are harmoniously focused by a leader through the company's vision that the edges are focused with maximum impact in a chosen market. The vision is manifested through an intensely-managed wedding of the company's culture and overall competitive strategy.

Innovation in each of the wedge's components is essential for maximum impact, and the design principles express how innovation occurs within those components. The assumption is that many of these principles can be useful to other companies. Briefly, these principles are:

Compete Globally to Succeed Locally—you don't have a corporate strategy unless it includes how to compete successfully in the emerging global economy.

Innovate, Innovate, Innovate Continuously—preserve a "Start Up Mentality" at all costs.

Preserve a Bias toward Growth—very simply, the organization that stops growing dies.

Work against Boundaries—test limits and assumptions in every facet of the organization.

Create, Not Just React, to Your Environment—proactively manage those things most critical to your success.

Nurture Self-Designing Behavior—create opportunities and space for people and groups, sharing power and using trust as design principles.

Don't Just Accept, Embrace the Primacy of Technology—you have to master technology and control it, even regain control of it if you've lost it.

Some of these points appear obvious, others less so. The point to *Sweet Success* is that NutraSweet is an example of a company which is struggling and winning in applying these principles.

While so much of this book focuses upon NutraSweet, it is important to conclude in Chapter 9 by expressing some of the unresolved policy challenges facing the company and our government. Government policy and intervention obviously play critical roles for firms in the food and pharmaceutical industries, and the emergence of the whole global biotechnology industry poses tremendous ethical, public perception, and competitive challenges as many, many more billion dollar businesses become visible. How these challenges are faced affects our very health and the role of advanced technologies in feeding the world.

Joseph E. McCann

ACKNOWLEDGMENTS

The idea for this book came from a dinner conversation between John Robson, then my dean at Emory and now Deputy Treasury Secretary, and Bob Shapiro, CEO of The NutraSweet Company. The more I heard of their times together, the more I became convinced that their story was worth telling. I am grateful to both of them for supporting this effort, and for Max Downham's superior coordination.

A tremendous number of NutraSweet folks contributed time and ideas to this book. In Augusta, the list includes almost too many individuals to name but certainly includes Ralph Bietz, Dave Sharp, Paul Givens, Woody Stiles, Mike Newcomb, Dave Easterly, Bobby Mims, Rhonda Easler, Jim Reese, Lito Castelo, Billy Adams, Doug Padgett and Foy Roberts. In Deerfield, Tom Burnet, Gerry Gaull, Lou Goldsmith, John Grove, Barry Homler, Mike Losee, Kevin Krail, George Logan, Don Minarich, John Witt, Dave Morley, Linda Gohlke, Nick Rosa, Frank Kotsonis, and Diane Moloney offered excellent insight and assistance. Outsiders include Ian Miller at Olgivy & Mather, Jim Phelps and Roger Thies in Washington, D.C., Dan Searle in Skokie (who is a quiet hero in many respects in this story), and Steve Ste. Marie at Egon Zehnder. At Emory, my research assistants included Tacy Underwood, Jeff Grosman, Michael Feder, with editorial support from Roger Heisler and collegial support from Rob Kazanjian. My son, Trent, also served heavy duty as a research assistant one summer.

J. E. M.

CONTENTS

CHAPTER 1

CHALLENGES—PAST
AND FUTURE

> Most people around this company hear a clock ticking.
> —*Bob Shapiro*

NutraSweet is a company in a big hurry. Everyone from the forklift driver in the Augusta, Georgia, plant to Bob Shapiro, NutraSweet's chief executive officer (CEO), knows how big that hurry has to be. With the use patent for aspartame expiring in 1992, there is precious little time to complete execution of the corporate strategy that has been emerging over the past six years. For Monsanto, which acquired G. D. Searle & Co. and the NutraSweet Company for $2.8 billion in 1985, NutraSweet's fate is also of special concern. With patents outside the United States expiring in 1991 on Roundup, its own core product, Act Two at NutraSweet is going to have to be a smash. Profits from aspartame and Roundup have accounted for 30 to 40 percent of Monsanto's profits. Third-quarter 1989 profits also reflected NutraSweet's importance. Monsanto's sales were flat on the chemical side, but NutraSweet's 40 percent increase in net profit made its performance the best in the chemical industry for that period. First quarter 1990 profits from chemicals were also down for Monsanto, again emphasizing NutraSweet's importance.

For a company based on making what insiders call "90-yard passes in tight spots," NutraSweet's future success will depend more on learning to play a "great running game"—fewer big gains and a lot more concentration on making first downs. Many of the lessons learned with aspartame are helpful; some are not. A major premise of this book is that the playing field for innovation in the 1990s and beyond is fundamentally changing—it's a global, intensely competitive environment with high stakes not only for NutraSweet but for every technology-intensive American firm. How a firm competed in the past is not only a poor guide for the present but may be seriously flawed as a guide for the future. The future is up for grabs and has to be designed using still vague and untested principles.

This book is not simply a story about another unique and successful new product introduction. It is a great story with much to learn from it, as Chapters 2 through 6 will illustrate. More important, NutraSweet serves as an important source of learning about how to design organizations capable of successfully innovating to compete on this new playing field. This cannot be just a happy face account of one more corporation's doing well. Aspartame has had a controversial past, and the very future of food will depend on how well companies like NutraSweet go about their business. In many ways, it is a story about the state of American technological innovation, and what one company is learning and is now willing to share with others.

Understand, however, that NutraSweet is moving from a position of strength. With 1988 sales of $736 million and net operating income of $154 million, a number that reflects heavy R&D spending, charges against income by Monsanto, and investment in manufacturing capacity, there are plenty of resources to do what is needed. The year 1989 was even better, with operating income of $180 million, up 16.8 percent, on sales of $869 million, up 18 percent.

To understand just how successful NutraSweet is, try these numbers. Using 1987 net sales of $722 million and $145 million in operating income, NutraSweet would rank as an independent company 385th in sales, 158th in operating income, and 9th in profitability as a percentage of sales compared to the Fortune 500.[1] These numbers mean that the company had had up until then a 143 percent compound annual growth rate and operating earnings, a 127 percent rate. Not bad for a company that was allowed to sell its one product only six years earlier.

Yet the sales for any single year haven't exceeded $1 billion, and the title of this book suggests that sales have done precisely that. The $1 billion number reflects the fact that combined sales for previous years have exceeded this figure a couple of times over, and that NutraSweet, in its usual optimistic style, plans on hitting the $1 billion mark shortly. Throw in competitors' sales and you are even closer to that figure. Most remarkable, however, is the impact aspartame has had in increasing the sales of food companies which have adopted it. NutraSweet has contributed to the growth of markets well beyond the billion-dollar range for several of the best known companies in the world.

With approvals in 79 countries, NutraSweet brand aspartame is now used in over 2,000 products, and major new applications clear the FDA each year. Three fourths of all Americans have tried NutraSweet brand sweetener, with 98 percent able to identify NutraSweet from a list as a sweetener, and a striking 70 percent able to name it without prompting as a sweetener for foods and beverages.[2] Every manufacturer in the world works for that kind of brand recognition and acceptance. Few are able to achieve it to the point that people are willing to pay a premium for their product—particularly a food ingredient. The "branded ingredient" strategy is uniquely responsible for this success, and how it was executed is not only an interesting but controversial story told shortly.

NutraSweet spent over $60 million in the first three years on advertising. It has also tried to work closely with users like General Foods, the Coca-Cola Company, and PepsiCo to gain acceptance of products featuring its little red swirl logo and company name. The strategy has had an incredible impact. For example, remember dumping cups of sugar into those containers of grape Kool-Aid as a kid? Tasted great, of course, but your Mom and dentist knew that the stuff was eating holes in your teeth. Sales were showing it; the powdered soft drink market was shrinking 3 to 6 percent each year before NutraSweet. In the three years after switching to NutraSweet, sales had increased 40 percent, generating over $300 million a year in new sales for NutraSweet customers, and replacing about a billion pounds of sugar—mostly in kids' diets.[3]

The Coca-Cola Company and PepsiCo haven't always been ardent fans of the NutraSweet Company, as Chapter 5 reveals. Yet the simple fact is that NutraSweet has helped make the diet soft-drink business the fastest growing segment in what was once a stagnant market. By the year 2000, the diet segment of the industry is conservatively estimated to be at least 50 percent of the total soft drink market. We're talking about a *very* big market in which a one point market share gain had traditionally translated into $250 million more in sales.

But aspartame isn't cheap when compared to sugar, and particularly when compared to saccharin—25 to 35 times more expensive, in fact. This raises hell with the economics of soft drinks, needless to say. But Coca-Cola and PepsiCo were trapped with diet drinks using saccharin and cyclamate—both then under heavy attack. Aspartame was, and still is, the only sweetener scientifically tested as safe and approved by the FDA for soft drinks in the United States. As every secret taste test after taste test was proving to these companies, aspartame also tasted very much like sugar.

They now know that NutraSweet pays for itself by contributing to brand success—NutraSweet helps sell product. In fact, the Coca-Cola Company feels so confident about Diet Coke's number three place in the market, and the long-term trend toward even greater use of diet products, that in 1989 it chose to take on PepsiCo's sugar-based product, Pepsi, head-on.

With impact like that, then, who could question the future success of the NutraSweet Company? Answer: many, including both existing customers and a hopeful swarm of domestic, Asian, and European competitors. Without hesitation, the great majority of NutraSweet's customers will acknowledge the positive impact that its product has had for their businesses. On the other hand, to say that many of them are also looking forward to 1992 is an understatement.

Aspartame after 1992 will be cheaper; the price of aspartame in Europe where NutraSweet already faces competition is generally 30 percent less. As promised, U.S. prices are already falling in anticipation of 1992 and the increased manufacturing capacity coming on-line. Faced with chronic capacity shortages in the face of exploding demand, NutraSweet was not only priced high, but was also forced to limit product to individual users in the early days. You antagonize people when you do that, and some of them aren't used to that kind of treatment. Roger Enrico, author along with Jesse Kornbluth of *The Other Guy Blinked: How Pepsi Won The Cola Wars,* said about the situation facing him as the new head of Pepsi-Cola USA:

> Aspartame. Today it is one of the greatest things that ever happened to me. During my first 180 days, it was one of the worst. Aspartame taught me how *not* to lead. Today you see aspartame

on every can of diet soda you buy. In 1983 you didn't. Then you only saw saccharin. All aspartame was, at that time, was a pain in the neck to people like me.[4]

Still, economists can look at this situation and observe a classical, yet temporary, monopoly pricing situation due to the use patent. Their recommendation for NutraSweet would be simple: price high and take the "excess rents" and run. Where, though, and how do you position yourself for that day when the entry barrier drops and you may still want to be in that business? Classic competitive strategy à la Michael Porter would dictate either becoming the low-cost producer, get ready to defend niche segments, or get out.[5]

A strong brand name offers some hope of protection, based upon the company's European experience, but the transition to a low-cost producer is still traumatic for an organization dedicated to a "start-up mentality" and used to high margins. It is a lot less fun for people used to being shot from the sling-shot of rapid growth to grind out savings measured in pennies per kilo. The culture which was the source of success begins to change as people begin drifting away. Inevitable? That's an interesting question which occupies a lot of thinking these days in Deerfield, Illinois, NutraSweet's headquarters.

There are many single-product firms which streak across the sky like meteors and disintegrate because of their inability to make the needed transitions. Aspartame's discovery as a sweetener was, after all, an accident in a Searle lab. Pharmaceutical firms are used to the boom-bust cycle of drugs with, and then without, patent protection. You get in and then out of a business, particularly when it is as alien to your history and culture as the food industry was to Searle. And with Monsanto as a new parent in 1985, the commitment to the food business was even less clear.

Our whole modern business culture has become preoccupied with the short term. Mergers, acquisitions, and "portfolio balancing" divestitures become instruments that work against taking a long-term stand in a business in which the fundamentals are about to abruptly change. It would be easy to declare, "Great while it lasted, but now let's find other things to do."

Wrong. NutraSweet and Monsanto are totally dedicated to a long-haul presence in the food industry. Not just for sweeteners, either. Their commitment is based upon a fundamental redefinition of the business in which the company will compete. Bob Shapiro is quite prepared to help define not just his own company's future, but also that of the entire food industry. He is convinced that NutraSweet's existing pharmaceutical culture and standards, coupled with Monsanto's capacity and commitment to R&D, are very capable of creating what the corporate strategists call "sustainable competitive advantage."

This is an abstract way of saying that they are prepared to reshape the competitive dynamics of an entire industry historically lacking those same orientations. NutraSweet, and a few other pharmaceutical companies like Pfizer, are bringing to the food industry deep bio-engineering expertise and a comfort with tweeking numbers four decimal places beyond normal food-industry quality control limits. On the one hand, you're talking about designer molecules, while on the other, most innovations in taste and texture historically came from test kitchens. Quickly emerging is the "high-tech food" company which blends advanced technology with marketing in very creative ways. Not a trivial event, since the very future of food is at stake. As Bob Shapiro put it:

> For a technology company, we're pretty good on the marketing side. And for a marketing company, we're pretty good on the technology side. There are better technology companies than us, and there are better marketing companies than us. But we think that the intersection of marketing and technology holds very few companies that are good at both. And that's where NutraSweet is positioned. The next question is, are there enough products to be developed at that intersection that will sustain a company like ours. That's what we hope to find out in the coming years.[6]

While a desirable vision, the big question is whether there is enough time to bring it about. Simplesse, or "fake fat" as it has been called, is certainly promising, but it is still very early to say whether it can surpass aspartame's success. True, Kraft did fold its cards in the race to develop its own version of a fat substitute by placing the first order for Simplesse in August 1989. Olestra, the Procter & Gamble Company's entry, is still tied-up in additional tests because of health concerns.

To be successful, however, it will be absolutely essential for NutraSweet to also understand how to manage the cultural and organizational transition from a single-product firm built around a lab accident to something much broader and lasting. The shift to a multibusiness strategy and structure is fundamental and potentially traumatic. Without question, many of the lessons learned with aspartame are useful in guiding this transition. But everyone in the company knows that Simplesse and other yet unknown future discoveries will require doing new things in still unknown ways. Needed is a company capable of designing itself and its future on the run. NutraSweet and other American firms must learn not only from their pasts, but must also be able to learn continuously as the dynamics and dimensions of a global competitive innovation race quickly unfolds.

The new playing field for innovation never existed as fully for Searle in the early days of aspartame's discovery as it now does for NutraSweet. Approximately 20 years have elapsed! Flourishing in this environment will require applying design principles at the very edge of what we know about leading people and designing innovative organizations in a global economy.

To help make sense of the aspartame story, it is useful to first put corporate technological innovation in context using a simple model. Alfred D. Chandler, the Harvard Business School professor, demonstrated the power of the historical perspective when he charted the developmental path of several large American firms. His landmark books, *Strategy and Structure* and *The Visible Hand,* illustrate the importance of key transition events and strategic choices on the subsequent development of the firm.[7] G. D. Searle & Co. is no exception. The critical transition points in its history need to be understood since they determined the menu of strategic choices available to its leaders when aspartame's use as a sweetener was discovered. Much of this chapter deals with those very critical early days for this reason.

THE CONTEXT OF CORPORATE INNOVATION

It could be comforting to think that all significant discoveries within business spring from systematic science—science proceeding methodically and confidently from a known knowledge base to a relatively known end. Societal development and corporate success would be assured in such an orderly world. In fact, most product extensions and modifications, along with a great many new products, do follow this path which Steven Schnaars calls "intentional innovation."[8] It is this path that helps prolong a product's life, or provide that few percentage points of difference in manufacturing costs which gives competitive advantage and market share.

On the other hand, this was not the initial innovation path for aspartame. Aspartame is what I call an "exploited surprise." It was serendipity, luck, chance, whatever you may call it, at the time of its discovery. But the larger innovation context in which it was discovered was far from that. The American pharmaceutical industry, like other technology intensive industries, tries to practice intentional innovation in its most rigorous, systematic form.

The Food and Drug Administration (FDA) is charged with protecting America's food supply, and has always found it easier to say no than yes when it comes to approving a new drug or food additive. A host of consumer "watchdog" groups have also sprung up to monitor both the industry and the FDA. While conditions like those described by Upton Sinclair in *The Jungle*[9] are only bad memories for the food industry, even today there is genuine concern about this industry's ability to regulate itself. It is prone to hype and misleading advertising, particularly about the health benefits of products. The line between drug companies and food companies continues to blur. This blurring is one of the most important, and potentially controversial, future trends to impact the American public.

Pharmaceutical firms like Searle and the other food industry giants certainly don't want to intentionally hurt people for the sake of profits, yet the very complexity of the scientific process, coupled with inherent flaws in the regulatory structure, can damage people. The pharmaceutical and food industries, like no other industries today, are the interface between citizens and the cutting edge of technology. Regulating that interface has got to be one of the most difficult tasks ever conceived.

While nice surprises like aspartame do come about once in a great while, the innovation machinery created within these firms must quickly, efficiently, and astutely come into play once the potential value of such a surprise becomes known. Success is therefore ultimately measured in terms of how well you manage this process. Despite the best intentions of its creators and participants, managing the maze-like regulatory process involves much more than conducting "good science" alone.

Like many others in this intensively competitive, often very profitable industry, Searle had been totally dedicated to the systematic discovery and exploitation of products derived from massive expenditures of R&D dollars. When successful, it was privileged by patent protection which allowed it to reap very substantial profits for several years. These profits are supposed to compensate the firm for the risks it assumed in spending those dollars in a calculated gamble.

If not successful, however, the product pipeline can dry up, patents eventually expire, and profit margins plummet as competition enters and the products "go generic." The firm dies unless it figures out what else it can do well. This cycle was repeated more than once in Searle's history, and it has had lots of company as others in the industry ride their own boom/bust product-innovation cycles. Learning how to place and manage very large R&D bets in this innovation race therefore becomes a critical success factor in this industry.

A basic premise is that any firm has to be good at more than one form of innovation in today's emerging competitive innovation environment. While a firm may be better in one form of innovation than another, one form will not sustain it indefinitely. Executives in these firms understand this fact, and they are actively trying to build a balanced innovation posture.

NutraSweet Company is developing both innovation capacity and competence as quickly as possible, but the history of Searle, like that of a great many American firms, had been punctuated by episodes of imbalance and distraction from the innovation process. In Searle's case, the firm chose to diversify into a number of related businesses and expand aggressively abroad. These strategies created such complexity that management had difficulty juggling the needs of each of the businesses, particularly the new drug innovation process. A simple matrix is presented to better understand the variety of innovation forms that are possible.

THE INNOVATION MATRIX

As Figure 1–1 illustrates, innovation can occur in both how something is produced—that is, in the process technology used to create a product—and in the uses for the product created through that process. Patents are granted for both types of innovations: process patents and use or application patents.

The distinction between these two basic forms of innovation is far from trivial, particularly in the case of aspartame. Aspartame's use as a sweetener was the result of an intentional innovation process its creators were engaged in while looking for something entirely different; a sweetener was the last thing they expected. The patent NutraSweet obtained is a use patent. While extremely complicated to make, the chemical compound aspartame can be, and is, created by other firms, but its use as a sweetener belongs to NutraSweet until 1992. NutraSweet lacked the know-how and capacity to develop much of its own commercially viable process technology until several years later.

FIGURE 1–1
The Innovation Matrix

| | Knowledge about Its Uses | |
	Known	Unknown
Known	Intentional innovation Cell A	Exploited surprises Cell C
Knowledge about How It Works **Unknown**	Process innovation Cell B	Pure research Cell D

Intentional Innovation

Cell A is the innovation path described by Steven Schnaars—intentional innovation directed at known processes and existing products with known uses. This is the battleground on which manufacturers around the world are now most visibly competing. Is it possible to get on a plane these days without sitting beside someone who has just been or is heading to a "total quality" education program of some type? Please, I'm not complaining about being bored on my trips. To the contrary, I'm ecstatic! Firms are looking for quality and productivity gains in their manufacturing processes anywhere and everywhere they can find them. American manufacturing is making a comeback!

There is absolutely no question that American firms are taking productivity and quality innovation seriously. A 1989 survey of large U.S. industrial firms by Organizational Dynamics, a management consulting firm, revealed that 87 percent of these firms were planning on expanding their quality enhancement programs.[10] I also particularly love Jim Robinson's, American Express' CEO, often-used quote about the importance of quality: "Quality is the only patent protection we've got."[11] NutraSweet has certainly caught on to the need for Cell A innovation to become the low cost/high quality producer for aspartame as 1992 nears. How it is doing so is the focus of Chapter 4.

The Japanese practiced and still excel in Cell A innovation. The Japanese term for this type of effort is called *kaizen,* meaning ongoing improvements in the product or process.[12] To illustrate the impact of this form of incremental innovation, JVC, along with Sony and Matsushita, took a professional-use product initially costing $20,000 in the United States and turned it into a $1,500 product. This product is, of course, the videocassette recorder. The Japanese now effectively control this multibillion dollar world market. This is not the only product area where we have given up ground. Table 1–1 lists several others.

It is uncomfortable to remember that this type of innovation was once a strong domain of American business. The concepts and methods used in this battle were pioneered by the early

TABLE 1–1
The Erosion of the U.S. Share of Technology Markets

Technology	Pioneered by	U.S. Companies' Share of Domestic American Market (percent)					Estimated 1987 Value of U.S. Market ($ millions)
		1970	1975	1980	1987		
Phonograph	United States	90	40	30	1		630
Television							
Black and white	United States	65	30	15	2		175
Color	United States	90	80	60	10		14,050
Videocassette recorder	United States	10	10	1	1		2,895
Ballbearings	Germany	88	83	71	71		41,657
Machine tools, machine centers	United States	100*	97*	79	35		485
Telephone sets	United States	99	95	88	25		2,000
Semiconductors†	United States	89	71	65	64		19,100

*Estimates.
†Data is for semiconductor merchant only. U.S. company share includes production of foreign subsidiaries operating in the United States.

Source: International Trade Administration, U.S. Department of Commerce.

management scientists like Frederick Taylor, and later by Will Juran and W. E. Deming.[13] It is reassuring to know that we've begun remembering those lessons. Americans can also be incredibly effective in Cell A type innovation, but several factors weighed-in against us over the past 30 years which helped atrophy those skills until very recently.

As Alfred Chandler and even earlier historians have pointed out, managerial innovations in analytic technique, organization design, and information technologies can pave the way for major changes in the way firms think about their businesses. The incredible impact of business portfolio theory advocated by such firms as the Boston Consulting Group has been one of these innovations. The development of what institutional economist Oliver Williamson and management professor Bill Ouchi call the "M Form", multidivisional organization structure is another example.[14] Coupled together, these two managerial innovations have, on the one hand, allowed us to create incredibly large and complex combinations of businesses. On the other hand, they helped create organizations that are very often too large, too diverse, and too short-sighted to be viable in today's competitive climate.[15]

The classic Boston Consulting Group matrix, for example, arrayed the firm's businesses as an investment portfolio which was changed to achieve specific growth and market share goals. Businesses were acquired and sold, often in relatively short periods of time, to meet short-term financial performance measures. Churning businesses in a portfolio based upon return on investment, without adequately investing money in them to build their long-term performance potential, is simply crazy. Is it done? Of course, but hopefully much less than in the last decade.

The multidivisional structure facilitated this process by allowing firms to be added and spun-off with theoretically minimal disruption to the rest of the firm. This combination of managerial innovations has been increasingly criticized, and the move back toward simpler, more focused organizations has rapidly accelerated.

In terms of their impact on corporate innovation, the effects have been lasting, perhaps even fatal for some firms which have been acquired or merged because their own growth prospects were not bright. Why invest in manufacturing and engineering activities to improve efficiency or product quality when you can readily sell that business and avoid the investment? Is it possible for a firm to become an "acquisition junkie" which needs to make acquisitions because it is unable to internally innovate? As I pointed out in my book, *Joining Forces*, there are, of course, many excellent reasons to effect mergers and acquisitions, but there must afterwards also be a total, unwavering, long-term commitment to perfecting the competitive capacity of an acquisition.[16]

The swing back from conglomeration has the potential of going too far. There is a growing belief that a company can be just as, if not more, effective by collaborating with other companies through joint ventures and alliances. The company "jobs-out" or externalizes activities and tasks to other companies with which it networks, internally retaining only those tasks which are the most critical and value-creating for customers. The risk is that the firm does not internally develop the knowledge and skills necessary to perform many of these activities and tasks. While appealing from an efficiency perspective, the return to more market and network forms of organization through this externalization process creates many new interdependencies that must be managed. The company potentially loses control of its future to others. It was this uncomfortable prospect for NutraSweet that resulted in its building an internal capacity to manufacture aspartame.

Similarly, the arrogance of some managements about the ability of their firms to dictate product acceptance by customers has been disastrous for their firms and industries. The obvious example is the American auto industry. Most of us would like to think that the Big Three have learned their lessons about being close to the customer and investing early and deeply in manufacturing. Whether this faith is justified or not can be argued.[17]

The essential idea in Cell A innovation is to take existing products and process technology and then ruthlessly and continuously innovate anywhere and everywhere you can to improve their usefulness and profitability. Companies are beginning to accept the idea that progress will come not through breakthroughs but from slugging it out each day on the shop floor and office. Understand, however, that individual gains can be very small, but when applied to an entire production process and product line the results can be dramatic, if not transforming. Continuous attention to process improvements eventually means that you will expand the scope of your attention to entire manufacturing and management systems. As later chapters will point out, the firm is ultimately transformed and becomes centered about the task of continuous product and process improvements.

Process Innovation

Cell B is the residence of some of our most well-known and admired innovations. Eli Whitney's cotton gin and Robert Fulton's steamboat are examples of process innovations, breakthroughs in how something is done, which dramatically improved the known uses for products created by their innovations. The cotton gin improved the quality and quantity of cotton growers could produce, while the steamboat made it possible to go places and at times not experienced until then. Most recently, new splicing and recombinant techniques in bio-engineering are creating products to better detect disease and improve plant strains. In Cell B, it is the process technologies for engineering disease-resistant plants that are the focus for innovation, not their uses.

One of the nicest stories told later in this chapter is about how Searle dramatically succeeded at this form of innovation. A decision was made far down in the firm by a single researcher, Lou Goldsmith, to try to regain control of the process technology used to make aspartame. Lou bootlegged money to develop the firm's own process technology for a key aspartame ingredient, *L-phe,* in a declining plant in Harbor Beach, Michigan. In doing so, he helped wrest control of the product's future back from Ajinomoto Company. This book could simply have been one more story about how the Japanese gained control of still another American initiated innovation without Lou Goldsmith and a handful of other Searle Company and later NutraSweet managers' willingness to do the new and unexpected.

Exploited Surprises

Cell C contains innovations which are new applications for products generated from known processes. These applications typically cross business or industry lines and are therefore new to that business or industry. As Steven Schnaars also notes, many of today's great innovations are of the Cell C variety.[18] It was Texas Instruments in electronics (not an existing slide-rule business) that introduced the calculator. Also, Federal Express, not UPS or the U.S. Post Office, created the express mail concept. Courier services had been in existence, but never applied to such a mass market so efficiently.

The hardest type of innovation to predict are those found in Cell C. While a radically new use for a product is frequently found, I'm compelled to wonder how many important uses go undiscovered, unnoticed, and never exploited. Aspartame is not one of those, obviously. Planning for surprises is a good trick, but a state of mind can be cultivated so that "surprises" don't go unnoticed. Indeed some corporate R&D scientists may contend that there is no such thing as an "accidental" discovery. The firm's culture hopefully creates conditions and practices such that the mental state of its employees prepares them to notice and seize upon the unusual. They are prepared to run opportunistically with a surprise just to see what happens when they probe and poke it. Once the potential of a new use is seen, however, serious corporate R&D swings into place—systematic, rigorous, and committed, at least until its commercial potential becomes clear. Firms like 3M are known for their ability to exploit, if not engineer, surprises.

Bob Daugherty, one of Bill Gore's many early "wunderkids" in his Flagstaff, Arizona plant, personally related an excellent story to illustrate the mental orientation which takes surprises in stride. Teflon was being explored for a number of uses in the plant, including in an expanded, air-impregnated form. One day, Bob Gore, Bill's son, had a hot glob of the stuff stuck in his glove. Frustrated, he tried to throw it away, but it made a long string as it continued sticking to his hand. The long Teflon string gave him an idea about how to work with the Teflon to make industrial seals. While eventually a very profitable application, the use of air-impregnated Teflon for seals was important for another reason; it was the precursor to Goretex, the fabric which later made Bill Gore famous.

The discovery by Roy Plunkett, a Du Pont scientist, of Teflon in 1938 was itself an accident. Plunkett's discovery was kept secret all through World War II as he and a Du Pont team spent years figuring out what to do with this by-product of a lab experiment. Bill Gore was a member of this team, and he stayed in Delaware to start his own business after leaving Du Pont. Today, Teflon is best known in the kitchen, which, in actuality, accounts for only 5 percent of its use.[19]

Teflon is an interesting example for another reason, as well. The branded ingredient strategy for aspartame—giving it the NutraSweet name—may have been unique to the food industry, but Teflon provided an excellent earlier model from another industry. Tertrafluoroethylene doesn't have a friendly sound to the ear, nor did aspartame.

Pure Research

Finally, Cell D innovations are the realm of pure science in that totally new processes may be explored resulting in products with unknown applications or usefulness. Place cold fusion and superconductivity in this cell, as examples. Some known and many unknown physical and chemical principles are being twinked, twisted, and unraveled by scientists without a clear sense of the true usefulness of what they discover. Since this book is about applied innovation, this cell isn't explored further.

SUMMARY

Because aspartame is an example of an exploited surprise, and not an outcome of pure research, it is important to understand the circumstances which lead to a potentially important new use either being discovered or going unnoticed. In fact, it was this very issue which attracted me to NutraSweet in the first place. I was curious about the story of James Schlatter's own successful 1965 lab accident. How did this event occur, what was the corporate response to it, and how could firms like Searle produce many more exploitable surprises like that? Were there lessons for other American firms?

Along the way of probing into the dim recesses of 1965 organizational memory, I soon discovered that the "here and now" of innovation within NutraSweet is just as, if not more, interesting than that of those initial past events. The innovation matrix is a useful device for putting aspartame's discovery in the larger context of other forms of corporate innovation. While it was an exploited surprise which gave the company its life, NutraSweet Company cannot count on that process again. It is very active in the other innovation matrix cells as it races toward 1992.

CHAPTER 2

CHANCE AND PREPARED MINDS

Chance favors the prepared mind.
—*L. Pasteur*

The industry and a firm's historical context play incredibly formative roles in shaping the path of corporate innovation. I quickly learned that you have to understand both of these contexts before understanding how a surprise like aspartame was exploited. For all practical purposes, Searle in the 1960s and 70s was a firm with limited prospects as it struggled with maturing products and an ambiguous business focus. The success of aspartame has, at least on the surface, the appearance of pulling a rabbit from a hat just at the right time. Or so it seemed.

G. D. Searle & Co. up until 1977 was a family firm in the tradition of the great family corporate dynasties so common in American business history.[1] In 1977 the family troika running the firm went outside to bring Don Rumsfeld in as CEO, and while the family presence was certainly felt for the next few years, there is little question that the dynasty passed leadership to an outsider.

Dan Searle continues to be active in business through a small venture capital firm in Skokie, Illinois, only a few miles from Searle and NutraSweet's separate corporate headquarters. Sitting in his office on a warm Saturday morning several months ago, watching him calmly clean his pipe and listening to the story of the family's decision, has left a lasting impression on me. I knew I was hearing, and a momentary participant in, a unique episode in American business history.

There is an unwritten rule for professional managers entering a family-run firm: Be the second one in, not the first. The transition to professional management can be traumatic, and the often repeated pattern is for the first professional executive to get blown-out of the firm in short order. The change in culture is simply too abrupt, the values and attitudes too sharp a contrast for the first outsider to be effective. The family members won't be satisfied with looking over the professional's shoulder, eventually intervening in day-to-day operations.

Dan and Bill Searle and Wes Dixon, Dan and Bill's brother-in-law, deserve credit for the smooth transition that occurred. But the firm Don Rumsfeld found upon entering was a troubled one, and, as a consequence, his entry was particularly timely and welcomed. Nor was he a complete stranger to the Searle family. As the junior, four-term former Congressman from that district, his skills and values were already known. His campaigns had also been supported by the Searle's. Still, the transition was formidable due to the state of the firm. How it got to that point in 1977 is worth knowing. It will sound like a familiar story because it vividly illustrates the general evolution and restructuring of American business which has been occurring over the past 10 to 15 years. It's a pattern we should hopefully learn from.

THE EVOLUTION OF G. D. SEARLE & COMPANY

The "G. D." in G. D. Searle comes from the family patriarch, Gideon Daniel Searle, who combined a knack for business with an interest in drugs to start a drugstore business in Fortville, Indiana in 1888.[2] He was 22 years old. Gideon's early aptitude for building businesses was quickly revealed. He subsequently bought and sold this and another drugstore for a profit before settling into one in Anderson, Indiana.

Like many druggists of this age, he prepared several of his own remedies which he sold to local doctors and other druggists. The drug business was effectively unregulated during this time, and was decidedly local in scope. The industry up until the 1930s appeared to be, according to Frederick Betz of the National Science Foundation, "more like a medieval apothecary."[3] To call it an industry is probably an overstatement. As Henry Gadsden, a Merck executive in 1983, said about the industry's early days:

> You could count the basic medicines on the fingers of your two hands. Most of our products were sold without a prescription. And 43 percent of the prescription medicines were compounded by the pharmacists, as compared with 1.2 percent today.[4]

With the encouragement of Eli Lilly, himself the founder of a future great pharmaceutical firm, Gideon moved to Omaha to found a manufacturing company with a partner, Franklin Hereth. After relocating to Chicago in 1890 to get access to a larger market, Hereth sold his share of the company to Gideon in 1905. G. D. Searle & Co. was formed in 1908.

Gideon Searle died in 1917 after creating a special market niche in the upper Midwest for elixirs and salves marketed directly to doctors. Claude Howard Searle, Gideon's son and a doctor, had taken over the management of the company as Gideon's health failed, and pushed the firm into more chemistry-based research. German and other European companies were manufacturing drugs using chemistry, unlike American drugs which were based more upon plants. Chemistry in Europe was much further advanced than in the United States, and the first significant R&D breakthroughs were coming from German firms such as I. G. Farben. World War I had a tremendously positive impact on American pharmaceutical firms because it dramatically reduced imports of these European (mostly German) drugs. The research push payed off with significant new products in the 1920s and 30s.

It was Claude's son, John Gideon Searle, who assumed control of the firm as general manager in 1931. Like all the family members, John had had an opportunity to work in the firm and learn the business since childhood. The most significant challenge in the firm's history was left for him to confront— the Great Depression. His decisions about what to do with falling sales marked a major transition point for the firm. Rather than retrench and lay off employees, he performed a detailed product and market analysis which resulted in a smaller, yet more profitable product line that was to be marketed not just regionally but nationally. The dramatic expansion of geographic scope would be supported by more and continuous spending on research to keep a flow of very narrowly focused new products going. These moves came at a time when several other firms were moving in the opposite direction.

World War II accelerated the push by the U.S. government to support the growing pharmaceutical industry. Much of the basic research was coming from universities with government support. R&D spending by firms within the industry was never great, as a result. The government-sponsored infrastructure built during the war and research support did stimulate more R&D and product development during the 1950s.

Several decades of prosperity followed as John Searle rounded out his entrepreneurial talent with the professional management skills of Paul Tillman in finance, Dr. Albert Raymond in research, and Franklin O'Brien in marketing. This team not only allowed the firm to survive the Great Depression, but also to keep new products profitably flowing into expanding markets. Three of these products were Metamucil, Dramamine, and Bathine, a peptic ulcer treatment. The prosperity was capped in 1950 by a successful public offering of stock for the first time.

The 1950s also marked a major push into international markets, prompted by Tillman and supported by John Searle's two sons, Daniel and William. Wes Dixon, John's son-in-law, was given the responsibility of developing the foreign operations. These three individuals, Dan, Bill, and Wes, had been around the firm for years and quickly slid into operational control of the firm. By 1976, about one half of G. D. Searle's pharmaceutical sales were from foreign markets.

New products continued to be introduced, but the firm was outspending all other pharmaceutical firms in their development, and the hit-rate wasn't what it should have been. Although the firm made the Fortune 500 for the first time in 1968, reality had already begun to set in. The new product pipeline was drying up. During the 1960s, 80 percent of the firm's profits were coming from only three or four products. The FDA regulatory process was also becoming increasingly complex and backlogged. The industry norm was that 9 out of 10 drugs making it to the safety-stage trials fail, and it could take as long as a decade to get through the entire process. It was time to do something dramatic.

John Searle stepped down from the presidency in 1966, leaving the Harvard-trained Dan in that role. Dan, Bill, and Wes formed the managing troika for the firm as it thought through its strategic options. Their relationships among themselves were comfortable and familiar due to their long apprenticeships. John did remain as chairman, and took more than a passing interest in everything going on in the firm until he retired in 1972. Still, with greater freedom to experiment, the three executives initiated an aggressive strategy to increase R&D, maximize cash flow by reducing costs and cutting the 75 percent dividend payout ratio, and diversifying into other health related businesses.

G. D. Searle's 10-year-long diversification move took it into two major businesses: health supplies and hospital equipment. The acquisition of Will Ross Hospital Supplies proved particularly important because it included an optical business, Pearle Vision. Don Rumsfeld, in a brilliant move, would later make Pearle a separate business that would be sold at a nice premium.

Diversification was, of course, the dominant business strategy for a great many corporations during this time period. Many of these strategies paid off for these companies, and the results for G. D. Searle were initially impressive, as well. Overall sales rose from $113 million in 1966 to $712 million in 1975. Net rose from $23 million to $80 million. The firm had grown to a point where its size and complexity were becoming a serious concern to Dan, Bill, and Wes. Taking the firm to the next level was, Dan candidly admitted, becoming an increasing formidable challenge.

The FDA was also raising questions at the same time about the quality of Searle's science regarding a drug called Flagyl. Ralph Nader's Health Research Group had even asked for a product recall after an FDA review of the firm's research records turned up apparent data errors. Whether the FDA's concerns were justified or not, it was clearly time to find professional management to deal with this complex organization that the family team had created, but now had to run.

A GREAT DISCOVERY BUT LOUSY
LAB TECHNIQUE

In 1965 there were three groups of scientists located in the bowels of the firm's Pharmaceutical Research and Development Division: Clinical, Biological, and Chemistry. Each performed its own relatively clear tasks, with the Chemistry group charged with identifying molecules which either facilitated or interfered with human body chemistry. The other groups would then figure out the impact of drugs containing those molecules. The Clinical group was responsible for establishing the safety and efficacy of those drugs to the satisfaction of the FDA and the firm's own internal standards, even though this took years. The intense scrutiny of regulators and competitors makes scientific rigor and internal organization essential in pharmaceutical R&D. When these lapse even for a moment, the damage can be lasting, as we will see.

Located within the Chemistry group was a "prep chemist," James Schlatter, who had been asked to make compounds for a senior chemist studying the use of dipeptides in ulcer treatment. He was working with a combination of aspartic acid (L-aspartyl) and a form of phenylalanine (L-phenylalanine methyl ester), or *L-phe,* which were both naturally occurring amino acids. The L stands for left-handed, meaning they were mirror images of other molecules. Curiously, neither molecule was sweet in itself, and while there is a whole class of so-called L-sugars, aspartame, as this compound was called, was not one of them. Aspartame, for some still unknown reason, binds to the sweetness receptors of the tongue to produce a sweet sensation.

The popular story within the firm has it that Schlatter licked his finger to wet it to turn a page in a book which was on his workbench. On his finger was some of the aspartame. After tasting its incredible sweetness, Schlatter had that presence of mind so hopefully cultivated in corporate research scientists. He called the event to the attention of others in his group. It was Dan Searle who later called Schlatter's bit of serendipity "a great discovery but lousy lab technique." Schlatter eventually retired from Searle, becoming one more of the corporate scientists of American legend whose "accidents" created immense wealth for their companies and jobs for thousands of people.

The first and most critical question always asked about any new compound was whether it was unique enough to be patented. Aspartame had already been discovered prior to Schlatter's experience, but its use as a sweetener was not patented. Whether justified in doing so or not required "normal" pharmaceutical R&D to swing into play, which it did in earnest. Dan Searle formed two technical teams under Robert Chein, director of marketing research. One team was to develop an initial strategy for the regulatory process, and the other to explore the compound's commercial potential.

Both teams faced difficult tasks. The regulatory strategy team made an initial bad assumption by thinking of the compound as a combination of two naturally occurring amino acids, which would have accelerated the approval process. The commercial team suffered a problem common to all firms making accidental discoveries—knowing which "problems" the discovery was the best solution to. Out of the world of market possibilities, which ones should be attacked first? There were then few reference points. This team did a great job of generating plenty of options, but offered few solutions about where to concentrate the company's efforts.

The compound was estimated to be gram for gram about 200 times as sweet as sugar. Its sweetness meant that it could be diluted down to the level of sugar without the calories. So there was growing, although certainly mild, curiosity about its value. Remember that there are many such inquiries occurring within any R&D unit, and most of these typically end nowhere. Still, a quick market analysis revealed that the market for artificial sweeteners was already several billion dollars and growing, and dominated by only two additives: saccharin and cyclamate.

To be patented as a product, the firm had to prove that the compound, still yet to be named, was unique—it had to be a unique "composition of matter" for a product patent. Technically, the compound wasn't even "artificial," since the two amino acids are natural constituents of proteins. Initial study revealed that methanol, a natural by-product of food digestion, was also produced when aspartame was metabolized. Some foods were known to produce more methanol than aspartame. L-aspartic acid could be relatively easily produced. L-phe, on the other hand, was an extremely complex and rare amino acid. Efficiently producing sufficiently large quantities of L-phe and combining it effectively with L-aspartic acid were to be the obvious bottlenecks. The process technology needed to overcome these obstacles was not well-known and certainly not within G. D. Searle at the time. While aspartame's "naturalness" was very attractive from a regulatory and marketing perspective, it complicated the patenting strategy. The alternative choice was to patent its use as a sweetener.

More than 500 combinations of similar molecules were eventually explored over the next two years, and none were found to be superior to aspartame. Whether another compound would emerge or not from a competitor simply wasn't clear at the time. A use patent, the perceived safest choice, was filed for and granted. But it wasn't until January 1969 that the firm initiated the FDA approval process by beginning safety tests. With a 17-year patent life, the clock had started running. Searle's executives knew what happened to profits whenever a drug came off patent; aspartame would become a pumpkin in 1986. As the firm became more intrigued by its market potential, Dan Searle made the decision to spend whatever was needed to bring aspartame to market as quickly as possible. Still, no more than a half-dozen staff members were occupied with the project at this early stage.

THE DIETETIC SWEETENER MARKET
UP UNTIL THE 1960s

By 1970, sales of all artificial sweeteners had already reached several billion dollars.[5] While today's health craze was still only getting started in the 1960s, the concern about excessive weight, cavities, and the desire for sugar substitutes for diabetics, created a demand for alternatives to sugar. The use of artificial sweeteners by people with medical problems still made an attractive market for a pharmaceutical firm used to niche marketing. However, there was absolutely no doubt that it was the "fear of fat" that would later drive most of this demand. Thin was "in," fat was "out." Most products containing artificial sweeteners were, however, confined to over-the-counter drug stores and special dieters' sections in the super markets. Their use in diet soft drinks changed all of that by creating a huge market for these alternatives.

The two dominant choices were saccharin and cyclamate, with saccharin controlling over 80 percent of the market. Sweet 'N Low, a combination of saccharin, cyclamate, and dextrose, had been very successfully introduced in the mid-1950s by Cumberland Packing Company, then a small Brooklyn firm. It quickly came to dominate the retail and institutional markets. Cumberland remains a major competitor today in the "tabletop market," although its share has eroded.

Saccharin had been around since 1879 when it was discovered in the lab. A derivative of salts of ortho-benzo-sulfimide, saccharin was first commercially used as a sweetener around 1910. It met swift reaction to ban it by the then head of the agency which was a precursor to the FDA for reasons that were unassociated to its chemistry. Dr. Henry Washington Wiley objected to saccharin because he thought that it was misleading; he felt that consumers thought they were getting sugar, then perceived to be a highly desirable food ingredient. In fact, the name *saccharin* was derived from "saccharine" which meant "sugar containing." Still, the ingredient had proponents, including President Teddy Roosevelt, who used it in his chewing tobacco. It found even greater acceptance during World War II due to sugar rationing. Saccharin's biggest disadvantage was that it left a bitter aftertaste.

Cyclamate was first marketed as a sweetener in 1949 and in combination with saccharin in 1953. This combination was particularly attractive, since cyclamate overcame saccharin's bitter aftertaste. While more expensive than saccharin, the cyclamate-saccharin combination was cheap; so cheap that the soft-drink companies offering diet versions were making more money on those products than their products containing sugar. A happy situation, to say the least. Tab, Coca-Cola Company's first diet soft drink, racked up an amazing 6.5 percent market share worth about $2 billion in sales at its peak, despite a flavor which its loyalists described to be like "kerosene."

The good times came crashing to an end in 1969 when tests concerning cyclamate's cancer-causing potential produced what then appeared to be strong positive results. As I note in a later chapter, however, this evidence now appears suspect, and it would not be surprising to see cyclamate reintroduced in foods and beverages in the United States within the next few years. It is still used in Europe. But the banning of a product in the United States was historic at the time. It certainly caused Sweet 'N Low to be reformulated without cyclamate.

When saccharin also later became suspected in 1977 as a carcinogen, you would have thought the world had ended. For the 30 million people who routinely used Sweet 'N Low, and those consumers used to their Tab and dietetic desserts, it wasn't a happy time. For companies like PepsiCo and Coca-Cola, who had spent millions on massive and glitsy roll-outs of their diet brands, the prospect of another FDA ban certainly was not great news either. The idea that there would be no artificial sweetener on the market at all proved to be too horrendous. Congress, in an unprecedented move, intervened with legislation that put a moratorium on the FDA's ban, thus allowing the sale of saccharin to continue, although with a health warning. This moratorium has since been extended four more times.

INTO THE REGULATORY LABYRINTH

The FDA was clearly becoming more aggressive in regulating drugs and food additives. The very process which helped open up huge market gaps for aspartame in the 1960s now also had to be encountered by Searle as it went forward seeking approval for its own additive. No firm, not even the most scientifically sophisticated, began this process without careful planning. The regulatory apparatus that had emerged over a hundred years had become incredibly complex. Only the most professionally organized, staffed, and well-funded firms could expect to master the regulatory labyrinth with any predictable chance of success. Chapter 3 picks up the later events in the regulatory nightmare that would soon unfold, but it is worth pausing here to explain the evolution and basic structure of a regulatory process that has, to a very great extent, served Americans well.

Protecting the Nation's Food Supply

Food additives had been used even before Roman times to prolong the life of food and prevent its contamination. Many of these additives were natural, such as spices and salt. Others were chemicals that produced no ill effects unless used in the wrong proportions, or when used as improper substitutes for safer but more expensive or hard to obtain additives. It was also not uncommon for merchants to cheat consumers by misrepresenting ingredients. A 1202 proclamation by King John of England, for example, prohibited the adulteration of bread by mixing peas or beans in it. There were few standards for measuring or labeling food or drugs well into the 19th century.[6]

The mid-1800s saw an explosion of concern and legislation by Congress about food and drugs. The bureaucratic structure that had been created to study these concerns was simple and amazingly lean for the impact it had. The Agriculture Department had been created by Lincoln in 1861 and staffed with 10 people, including a commissioner, to help disseminate information about technological innovations that could help farm production. The first chemist in the department had been Charles Wetherill, who thus became the first head of what was one day to become the FDA. Peter Collier served in 1879 as Chief Chemist within a small department appropriately called the Division of Chemistry in the Department of Agriculture. Collier's role was important because he began to actively study food and drug adulteration, and his efforts helped produce more than 100 food and drug–related bills over the next 25 years.

The cause for concern was real. Hundreds of consumers were being poisoned, maimed, or killed by products that were created in very unsanitary conditions, or produced using dangerous chemicals. Upton Sinclair's story of Jurgis, the Lithuanian immigrant in *The Jungle* who tried to survive working in the meat packing houses of turn-of-the-century Chicago, is still a vivid memory for me. Muckrakers like Sinclair had their impact, because in 1906 the Food and Drugs Act and The Meat Inspection Act were passed to deal with conditions like those they described in their books. It is difficult to find many equally vivid magazine and newspaper accounts of these conditions because advertisers would routinely threaten to pull their ads from publishers in retaliation for printing stories.

The 1906 Food and Drugs Act was recommended for revision in 1933. A five-year long intense battle in Congress and the press ensued before passage of the landmark Federal Food, Drug, and Cosmetic (FDC) Act of 1938. Among its many provisions was one requiring predistribution clearance for the safety of drugs. Food additives were added to the approval process in 1958 through the Food Additives Amendment. This amendment also called for the FDA to issue regulations specifying uses of an additive. The specification provision is an extremely important one because it meant that firms seeking approval must seek it for prescribed uses, and any additional uses would also have to be approved. For aspartame, this meant that its use would be confined to specific classes of food. In fact, it would be General Foods Company that would first work with Searle to develop uses in "dry" foods.

Over the following 20 years, standards and procedures for gaining approval continued to evolve. Citizens panels were used, and a major study of 4,000 drugs previously approved under "GRAS" provisions were studied in 1966 by the National Academy of Sciences/National Research Council. *GRAS* stands for "generally recognized as safe," and applies to drugs, foods, and additives that were existing prior to legislation and had a history of use. Being able to claim an additive's status as GRAS is therefore a tremendous advantage in speeding a product to market.

The GRAS classification is another important one because it came to haunt NutraSweet years later when the firm applied for FDA approval for Simplesse, its fat substitute. NutraSweet assumed that Simplesse's GRAS ingredients would qualify the processed product also as GRAS. The FDA objected and slowed up its approval for two years. While GRAS status would be granted, the politically sensitive nature of food regulation today meant that NutraSweet should not have made such a strategic assumption. You don't announce a product without working the system first.

It is ironic that a great many foods and drugs given GRAS status, including refined sugar, would be given a tough time if they were now introduced for the first time into the approval process. Saccharin and cyclamate, for example, had been allowed on the market because they were ruled GRAS. Protests by regulators and legislators to the contrary, the politics of the regulatory process do become visible at times.

Despite the best intentions of regulators, there were hundreds of thousands of consumers, several food companies with millions of dollars at risk, and several additive manufacturers that would resist any attempt to ban a product without clear and convincing evidence. On the other hand, you have a host of health-conscious consumer groups, such as the very sophisticated Center for Sciences in the Public Interest (CSPI), aggressively intervening in the process. Gaining their support, or at least having their neutrality, becomes valuable because of their knowledge, media access, and willingness to legally intervene in the regulatory process.

The Nature of Scientific Inquiry

The critical question to be answered in the regulatory approval process has always been, "Is the drug or food additive safe?" This is a tough question to answer. Proving safety is much, much harder than it can sound. According to Gerald McCowin, director of FDA's division of food and color additives, "Congress has defined safety as a reasonable certainty that no harm will result from use of an additive. In our evaluation we examine to see whether the additive has any toxic effects, whether it may cause birth defects. Does it interfere with nutrition? Does it affect individuals with allergies?"[7] Who and how someone defines "reasonable certainty" is the fundamental source of the difficulty in the process.

Normal scientific inquiry is designed to test specific hypotheses, and out of the realm of all possible hypotheses about the effects of an additive, carefully controlled lab experiments with test animals can only answer one at a time. It is methodical, time-consuming, and incredibly expensive. The best answer is always stated as a negative. For example, "There is no significant relationship observed between the use of the additive at these dosage levels and the incidence of birth defects in test animals." You then proceed to the next test, and the next test, until all possible questions and concerns are answered in the same way.

You eat up hundreds of thousands of dollars in a test, and you can proceed only so quickly—the gestation period of lab mice can't be speeded up. Along this path, acceptable levels of usage do emerge. Governing the laboratory testing process is the Official Methods of Analysis of the Association of Official Analytical Chemists, a book containing more than a thousand pages of internationally accepted laboratory methods accumulated since 1895.

The questions of greatest concern to FDA scientists are defined, and the acceptable research approaches the firm can take in responding to them are negotiated in advance. Nonetheless, the common experience is to run tests, present data, and then be asked to run additional tests to answer questions that either didn't surface the first time, or were raised by the data that was just presented. You can never prove that a drug or food additive is safe in every instance and in every way. You can only prove that the product isn't *unsafe*, and the list of what you may have to disprove can grow even with the most careful planning and negotiation. Eventually, however, safety test results are submitted and approved. The firm is then asked to meet what has been called the *100-fold rule;* the additive is ruled safe for prescribed uses at a level that is no more than 1/100th of the highest level at which it was fed to test animals and did not produce any harmful effects.

OPTIONS AND EARLY COMMITMENTS

Those were the prospects facing the small team within Searle Food Resources, Inc., the vehicle that had been set up to take the product to market. They found a large potential market, with the only competing product in deep trouble with the FDA, and a complex but previously navigated regulatory process. Still, the food business was relatively unknown to this pharmaceutical firm. Making a drug which was perhaps only going to be used by a small number of people with a serious health problem was not the same as making an additive which would potentially impact every American. Drugs marketed through doctors and drug stores were one thing, a food additive was something else entirely. The distribution channels were different, and the volumes of product to be manufactured and moved through those channels was staggering for a firm used to smaller batch technology processes.

Having to do business with food giants like General Foods, Procter & Gamble, Kraft, and the soft-drink companies wasn't a pleasant prospect either. They were not about to open their arms wide to a new food additive without complete confidence in it, a time-consuming and expensive proposition. The simple fact was that aspartame looked like a good substitute, but it also would cost much, much more than sugar or any other known artificial sweetener.

Companies like The Coca-Cola Company and PepsiCo also had reputations for being tough negotiators with their suppliers, dictating price and terms to such an extent that you wondered why you ever wanted to do business with them in the first place. The answer was clear, however. They were who they were, after all, and acceptance by any one of them would virtually guarantee success and open the floodgate of acceptances by other companies. But if you did decide to do business with the food giants, and they with you, you needed to be sure you could service them well.

For Searle, that opportunity appeared light years away. It was mentally and operationally very much a pharmaceutical company, not a food company. The firm did have a small business set up within a division that was making food enzymes through a fermentation process, but not anywhere near the scale needed to do aspartame on a national basis, let alone internationally.

Indeed, John Searle, who was still chairman, wasn't at all supportive of the idea of manufacturing it. He preferred instead to license away the patent and use the royalties to fund drug-related R&D. It was Dan Searle who persisted with the idea of at least controlling the distribution and marketing of aspartame, even though the manufacturing capacity and know-how didn't exist within the firm at the time. For Dan Searle, aspartame was one more step toward a diversified business base.

With the regulatory compliance process gaining momentum, attention turned to sourcing the two amino acids, L-aspartic and L-phenylalanine. L-aspartic wasn't the problem; L-phe was. Obviously, sufficient quantities of aspartame needed to be produced for the safety tests, and to allow experiments to test potential applications. Getting into the market fast after approval would also require capacity. The near term solution was to work with another company to get those supplies until, if ever, the firm decided to manufacture them on its own.

Ajinomoto Company, the giant Japanese food company, had come into the scene at the time of the patent filing. Ajinomoto was widely regarded as the world leader in amino acid research and production. It came to dominate, for example, the monosodium glutamate (MSG) market despite the fact that it was Stauffer Chemical, a U.S. company, that had pioneered the technology. Stauffer's experience with MSG lingered in the minds of several Searle and NutraSweet managers over the years as a reminder of what happens when you lose control of a technology.

What Ajinomoto had going for it was a synthetic L-phe molecule produced using chemistry, not fermentation. Ajinomoto, in the classic Japanese style of learning from others, had reportedly first learned about aspartame's use as a sweetener from a paper presented at a scientific conference one of its scientists had attended in the United States. Searle had beaten Ajinomoto "only by a hair" in filing for a patent on its very own discovery. Ajinomoto then called Searle to ask if they could help in some way. Searle, not unlike other U.S. firms, was slow to learn the value of secrecy as a competitive advantage. They have since learned it very well.

Ajinomoto would prove to be a formidable partner. It was able to provide Searle with the first complete manufacturing process for aspartame, which was later called the *Z-process*. Searle may have had the use patent on aspartame as a sweetener, but Ajinomoto had the process technology on the scale needed to produce it. This is the obvious basis for a joint venture. The basic agreement which was eventually negotiated was far reaching. In return for access to the process technology, Searle would pay Ajinomoto royalties, and each would share in the other's research involving the Z-process. Ajinomoto would have an exclusive license for Japan. They agreed to jointly market aspartame in Europe and a few North African countries. NutraSweet would have the United States and Canada. The rest of the world would be a "free trade zone" in which both would compete.

The combination of Ajinomoto and NutraSweet has today become a formidable global competitor. Not surprisingly, aspartame would one day become the only artificial sweetener ever approved in Japan. To this day, NutraSweet still pays some royalties to Ajinomoto. On the other hand, the provision regarding the sharing of technology involving the Z-process would later prove to be critical in setting NutraSweet on a more independent future direction.

Today, there are two competing views about the Ajinomoto relationship. Max Downham, now head of Mission & Strategy in NutraSweet, and previously in charge of managing the firm's relationship with Ajinomoto, calls it "a good, cordial, healthy, reliable relationship." He acknowledges, however, that the two firms make good allies together, but separately would also make formidable competitors—another indicator of a good joint venture relationship!

Other NutraSweet people are more cautious. They view the reluctance, so characteristically Japanese, to share information about Ajinomoto's own internal activities as unsettling. When one firm is in a total dependency relationship with another as Searle was at that point, the potential risks and uncertainty inherent in the relationship demand information sharing. Ajinomoto's perceived unwillingness to share information in those first critical years simply made some Searle researchers so uncomfortable that it eventually drove one of them, Lou Goldsmith, to explore alternative process technologies for producing the critical L-phe. Nor was Lou convinced, in his own characteristically stubborn scientific way, that the synthetic approach was better than the fermentation approach. What followed would later prove to be one of the critical transition points in a still young story.

THE END OF THE BEGINNING

During this whole period of evaluating manufacturing options and building relationships, the safety testing process had proceeded. Inventories of aspartame had started to build in anticipation of approval. Even though it took a long time the approval process had proceeded well, and in 1972 the results of the safety tests were submitted for review. A formal petition for approval was filed in 1973. The petition was amended to limit the uses of aspartame because some tests results had not been finalized. A warning label requirement was also agreed upon because of aspartame's phenylalanine content. One in 15,000 people were found when tested at birth to lack an enzyme which allowed this amino acid to be metabolized. Requiring the warning label was acknowledged as a wise decision, although phenylalanine could be found in even greater quantities in other protein-based foods such as meat and milk.

Searle's cooperative attitude proved helpful, and FDA approval was granted for dry use in July 1974. The first sales were in France, not the United States, however. This was a tabletop product called Equa, the percursor to Equal. Ajinomoto had produced product in anticipation of approval, and this inventory was now stored in Skokie.

General Foods had bravely worked with Searle through the whole testing period in hopes that it would be the first to market products containing aspartame. GF was never able to lock up aspartame for its exclusive use, and would even have to wait in line once in awhile along with everyone else during those early days of short supply after the second approval. But the relationship between the two companies is still treasured within NutraSweet because of GF's willingness to work with the company when friends were scarce. It was GF, in fact, that gave Searle the NutraSweet brand name for one dollar.

Jubilation was short lived. Critics quickly emerged to challenge the approval. Dr. John Olney and James Turner filed objections in August 1974, and asked for a stay of the approval and a hearing because they felt aspartame caused mental retardation, brain lesions, and neuroendocrine disorders. Olney and Turner were well-intentioned individuals who had a general distrust of food additives and their impact upon consumers. This would not be the last time they were to intervene in the approval process. Their objections did come during an era of increasing involvement of consumers in the regulatory process. While FDA refused to stay the approval, it did agree to a swift internal administrative review of their specific complaints.

The administrative device to be used was called a Public Board of Inquiry, or PBOI. The PBOI consisted of a panel of three scientists agreed upon by all parties. Selection of the panel stretched into 1975, and the rules governing the PBOI were left seriously vague and open to legal question. For example, there were no stated rules of evidence. During this time, Searle had voluntarily withheld aspartame from the U.S. market.

At the same time, congressional hearings were underway about the quality of scientific research within the pharmaceutical industry. Searle had the misfortune of having the supporting data for its drug Flagyl questioned by FDA while these were underway. Searle's problem eventually turned out to be one not uncommon to research spanning several years and multiple groups within the firm—poor record-keeping and data management. Further complicating their situation was a more serious question about the safety of two other important drugs, Aldactone and Aldacticide. Here, too, supporting data did not fit other statistics in the records. After scathing criticism from Ted Kennedy in a July 10, 1975 Senate subcommittee hearing, Searle invited FDA into the firm for a full-scale review to clear the air.

About 20 investigators showed up and began to camp out in Searle offices in October 1975. To the horror of those who had worked so hard on the aspartame approval, and were still heavily involved in negotiations with the FDA about the PBOI process, the investigators chose to look at the aspartame records, not the records for the drugs which has spurred the whole inquiry in the first place. For aspartame, here, too, poor record-keeping was found, and apparent errors in the data detected.

That pretty well did it. On December 5, the FDA stayed the aspartame approval. While Searle called the stay "well intentioned, but unfair," it chose not to contest it. The firm would do what was necessary to once again prove aspartame's safety. And for the record, as several former key Searle executives pointed out to me, no Searle product was ever removed from sale, nor anyone ever indicted, as part of that inquiry. Has the record keeping and data management improved? Don't even ask.

But the regulatory nightmare was only beginning for aspartame. It would not be until 1981 that approval would once again be gained. And it would be entirely new leadership within Searle that would see it happen.

CHAPTER 3

NEW BLOOD, NEW WAYS

Bright people can do anything.
—*John Robson*

The flip-chart pages Dan, Bill, and Wes had filled pretty much expressed their fantasies and hopes. The troika, as Dan Searle called it, had realized in early 1977 that their shared leadership of G. D. Searle wasn't working as well as needed to manage the situation now facing them. It had proven hard to agree on objectives, and the perception was that the team couldn't make the timely, big decisions needed. Line managers and staff would "work the system" by going to the troika member most likely to give approval on something wanted. The members knew this, and saw it symptomatic of the need to create another leadership structure. None of the three saw themselves in the CEO role.

They had first quietly met over several weeks' time to generate a list of the characteristics of the new leader, and later to generate a list of potential candidates that best fit those characteristics. The goal was to be as open-minded as possible, but one name kept coming to the top of each of their own lists — Don Rumsfeld. Don had never really been far from anyone's mind, some insiders say. Dan had followed Don Rumsfeld's career since he first ran for Congress in the Republican 13th District in Illinois at the age of 29.

Don Rumsfeld's career had been meteoric. The handsome, Princeton-educated congressman attracted attention just as the Republican era was beginning. Resigning his congressional seat in 1969, he began to hold a succession of increasingly powerful positions in the Nixon and Ford administrations: director of the Office of Economic Opportunity, director of the Cost of Living Council during the Nixon wage/price freeze, ambassador to NATO, White House chief of staff, and finally Secretary of Defense.

Despite this promising career trajectory, Rumsfeld had never been financially well-off, and a stint in the private sector after the 1976 election began to look more and more attractive. It would allow him to regroup and rethink next steps. This career path would follow that of many senior government executives who would, like David Halberstam's "best and brightest," drift in and out of administrations in various positions over their entire careers.[1] The ivy league academic-government-business administrative elite had traveled this orbit for generations, and Don Rumsfeld had had the opportunity to see how it worked.

In a September 1979 interview in *Fortune*, Rumsfeld would admit that he had felt it was time for a career change even before President Ford's defeat.[2] He lectured briefly at Princeton, his alma mater, and at Northwestern. In the spring of 1977 Dan Searle approached him about taking the CEO position. He accepted in April and showed up for work in June. He was quick to point out that he took a five-year contract, a sign he believed of his intention to stay in the job long enough to do what was needed.

Rumsfeld knew that there were a number of notable differences between running a major government agency and a business. In many respects, running a business was easier. You were evaluated on performance, not as much on perceptions. You could also act more decisively. There were other similarities, as well. Both were big organizations, with complex problems. Both required coordinated action built around a consensus about priorities. To communicate those priorities and make sure that he was leading, not reacting, he was an avid memo writer, a practice for which Don's friend and protégé, John Robson, also became notorious. Don is quoted in the *Fortune* article as saying that the move from Defense to Searle was probably easier than the move from Congress to the executive branch. Without question, he meant to apply his lessons from government to Searle quickly.

RUMSFELD TAKES HOLD

While Don Rumsfeld assumed the role of CEO, Dan retained the title of Chairman. The family interests still needed protection.

This situation had the potential for disaster. What served Don well was his willingness to consult broadly across the firm, and to keep Dan, Bill, and Wes involved in the decision-making process. Dan admits that if Don would have asked the three of them to leave at that point they would have declined. As a compromise, the three family members moved their offices across the small plaza into another office tower. Don was still in a fishbowl, however. Dan recounts the story of how impressed he was with Don's ability to learn facts quickly. One incident particularly sticks in his mind. On their first flight to Asia to look at the firm's businesses there, Dan observed Don reading and digesting a thick, detailed book on Japanese emperors just to better understand the culture. Don's tendency was to immerse himself totally in the subject at hand.

Their confidence was also justified, they feel, because of Don's opening moves. Don had, for example, quickly formed five task forces composed of directors, managers, and outsiders around the issues that he perceived most critical from his earlier interviews. The facts were that Searle's research pipeline had gone dry, it had over diversified and lost control of some of its 30 or so businesses, and the FDA inquiry still underway was posing serious questions about the quality of Searle's science. Major changes had to be quickly made. By involving the troika in this learning process, he earned the mandate to proceed.

John Robson was brought into Searle in October 1977 as executive vice president for planning and regulatory affairs to help execute these changes. Robson and Rumsfeld had known each other since high school, both attending New Trier High School, an exclusive north shore school known for producing an exceptional number of corporate and government leaders. Robson had just served as chairman of the board of the Civil Aeronautics Board (CAB) and had begun guiding it through the airline deregulation process. Robson had followed his father to Yale, and had graduated from Harvard Law School in 1955. He had become a senior law partner in Sidley & Austin, one of the nation's largest law firms, after helping his previous law firm merge with Sidley & Austin.

His knack for dealing with large government bureaucracies had been honed from his positions at CAB, as general counsel and then undersecretary of Transportation, and as White House

Staff. What the 47-year-old Robson liked best was to change things, and he embraced the role of "point man" in restructuring Searle. The importance of the Rumsfeld-Robson combination shouldn't be obscure by this time; they had both attended ivy league schools, knew each other well, and knew the workings of government even better.

Rounding out the executive team was James Denny, who joined Searle in February 1978 after serving as treasurer for the Firestone Tire & Rubber Co. Denny, who was also incidentally a lawyer by training, would become chief financial officer and responsible for identifying how to improve Searle's financial performance. On the R&D side, Dr. Daniel Azarnoff, a highly respected academic and medical administrator, joined the management team in 1978. His task was to evaluate the R&D side of the business and get products moving again through the pipeline.

The team soon saw that Searle was fundamentally sound. The firm had a solid reputation with doctors, despite its present problems, and the balance sheet was equally solid. Performance was simply "masked," according to Robson, and the needed changes could reveal the true strength of the firm. They started in by restructuring the board of directors to bring in several well-known executives, medical authorities, and former government officials. Eleven of the 15 board members were now not employed by Searle, a further indicator of the move to a professionally managed firm.

Other changes also came quickly, including cutting corporate staff from 850 to 350 people, divesting 20 of the most marginal businesses, and repatriating significant earnings from their Puerto Rican businesses. Several of the divested businesses were joint ventures in Asia and Latin America. Robson was responsible for pulling Searle out of those ventures. Ironically, he would return to Central America years later as Deputy Treasury Secretary to find ways of putting a billion dollars into the Panamanian economy following the U.S. invasion in 1989. For Searle, however, he had to execute a refocusing strategy. The corporate strategy, so typical of the experiences of other overly diversified corporations at the time, was to refocus on the core business. Diversification, while so attractive a strategy initially, was proving to be somewhat operationally complex for corporate America.

A "bad news" policy was introduced which encouraged acknowledging difficulties with products and performance sooner. Quality assurance and regulatory affairs functions were also overhauled and upgraded in importance because of the FDA inquiry. Assisting Rumsfeld in this particular effort was another lawyer, Marty Hoffman, Rumsfeld's former college roommate and Secretary of the Army, who had a special knack for what Hoffman called "cleaning up messes."

Rigorous documentation and research protocols were instituted as part of the quality assurance program. A corporate-wide standards of conduct policy was created to visibly emphasize Searle's ethical business practices. At the same time, new financial controls and information systems had been introduced to support more decentralized management. Financial performance began improving dramatically after the first two years of restructuring.

"SCIENCE IS A MOVING TARGET"

The FDA's stay order had effectively put aspartame in limbo. The aspartame team that had worked for the first approval now faced a new question about how to proceed. FDA staff hoped to help by recommending in the summer of 1976 that Searle contract with an independent research consortium called Universities Associated for Research and Education in Pathology (UAREP). FDA would draft the contract, which Searle would pay for, and have UAREP review the most "critical" research studies conducted by Searle to validate their reported results.

While a positive suggestion, there was a real killer of an added provision, according to Roger Thies, then a Searle staff lawyer. Thies would later be assigned in 1979 to lead the team charged to find a way out of the impasse that would soon grow even larger. He had joined Searle in 1970, and had followed aspartame's path through the regulatory process for some time, but only from a distance. He had been there the day the 20 FDA investigators set up camp in Searle's hallways. To Thies, the

FDA was proposing a "two-horse contract." Not only would UAREP validate the Searle studies, but the contract would also call for UAREP to assist the FDA in the criminal investigation then underway within Searle. Awkward, especially since Searle was being asked to foot the bill. The two parts of the contract were eventually separated.

Time went by, and UAREP reported-out in the summer of 1977 on the first three of the Searle studies. Searle's test results were supported. UAREP then began to validate the additional studies, a process which would take many more months. UAREP, while slow, was at least proceeding with scientific rigor.

In December 1980, all other criminal investigations of Searle were dropped. The quality assurance changes that had been instituted under Rumsfeld also gave the FDA confidence that Searle's research would not be a problem again. In fact, another product-related problem would one day be encountered by Searle when some women suffered health problems apparently induced by its copper IUD. The embarrassingly bad and costly record keeping and research documentation mistakes had, at least, been overcome.

The Olney and Turner objections had yet to be considered by the Public Board of Inquiry (PBOI). It was 1978, and now additional new objections were also being raised by other critical researchers who said that aspartame caused brain tumors in test rats. The FDA maintained, however, that none of these objections could be heard by the PBOI until UAREP finished its work. The last of the UAREP validated studies were finally reported back to the FDA, and all results again confirmed the Searle data. Arguments over the rules to govern the PBOI process went on well into 1979, and it wasn't until June of that year that FDA Commissioner Kennedy finally announced agreement among all the parties. It was now 4 years since the stay was enacted, and 14 years since aspartame's use as a sweetener had been discovered.

Oral testimony began in January 1980. Keep in mind that this was the first time a PBOI had been used by the FDA. As it turned out, the testimony that was given would mix fact with the absurd. The lack of clear rules of evidence made it difficult to substantiate which was which. The public exposure of the process added to the confusion. The PBOI concept was turning out to be unwieldy, and would, just for the record, only be used one more time in the future by the FDA. The whole process was dragging out and no end was in sight.

Even with positive UAREP and PBOI findings, it was pretty clear within the Searle organization that the removal of the stay was going to draw intense public and political scrutiny. Given the bad press about the earlier FDA inquiry of Searle and the sensationalized media reporting that had occurred, the FDA could "take a dive," play it safe, and deny the removal of the stay even with positive UAREP and PBOI findings. Rumsfeld and Robson had become so demoralized that they actually approved writing-off the books about $21 million in aspartame held as inventory in anticipation of a go-ahead. The write-off would severely hurt Searle's reported profits for the year, but they felt that it was better to take the hit and get it over with.

Out of sheer frustration, Searle did the totally unexpected and unprecedented step of suing the FDA in October 1980. Just about every lawyer in Washington, D.C. had advised the firm not to do it. Sure death for all future product approvals, they told the company. But the new leadership in Searle was aggressive and, more important, willing to act on the basis of their convictions. Right was right, they felt, and the firm had bent over backwards to accommodate critics and the FDA. The suit called for the FDA Commissioner to expedite the process and make a decision, one way or another.

The idea of a lawsuit had the markings of a Rumsfeld/ Robson decision. The input of another recent addition to the Searle staff was not as visible. Robert Shapiro was 40 when he joined Searle in 1979 as general counsel and vice president. Shapiro had been educated at Harvard and Columbia Law School, and had worked primarily on labor and antitrust cases up to his appointment to several government transportation-related advisory committees and policy councils. His work in these areas, particularly on a CAB committee Robson had appointed him to in 1975, gave him, along with Rumsfeld and Robson, a special appreciation of the regulatory process.

Shapiro wasn't just a newcomer to business. He had become general counsel for General Instrument Corporation, a New

York-based conglomerate in 1972. He had immersed himself in its marketing and strategy areas for seven years before coming to Searle. His initial task in Searle was to shed the troubled hospital supply business, which he did well. He demonstrated the same energy and knack for business which Rumsfeld and Robson demonstrated. Searle had effectively become—in two of its top positions—a firm managed by lawyers. To everyone's pleasant surprise, Robson and Shapiro also had good business sense. For Shapiro, just how much business sense he had would soon become even clearer. In less than two years he would be named head of the NutraSweet division formed to take aspartame to market.

Searle management obviously had needed to maintain good communications with the FDA right at this point, because the decision to file a suit may have been different if they knew just how close the PBOI was to a conclusion. The three-person panel announced a decision only hours after the suit was filed. There is apparently no connection between the suit and the timing of the PBOI's decisions. The panel held that aspartame did not pose a risk of retardation, neuroendocrine disorders, or brain lesions. In a surprise move, the panel concluded that the possibility of brain tumors could not be ruled out, and recommended another study at *lower* dosage levels, an unheard of research practice.

The suit remained there while everyone tried to figure out what to do with this new twist. The critics had again filed objections, this time about the validity of the research data. Searle and the Bureau of Foods filed exceptions about the request for another study. The Bureau of Foods, it should be noted, was the actual defendant throughout this whole process because it had technically granted the first approval. The situation was moving into limbo once again. Finally, the judge hearing the suit told the FDA to either decide or a summary judgment would be made.

The FDA Commissioner agreed to the PBOI's first decision, and reversed the second one because the PBOI panel had actually made factual and statistical interpretation errors for the rat tumor data. Another independent study on the brain tumor question had also been completed by Ajinomoto since then, and it had found no connection either. Commissioner Arthur Hull Hayes issued his final approval on July 15, 1981. No appeals were filed by objectors.

Criticisms and objections about aspartame would continue to surface for another six years, however. None of these were to prove as damaging as this six-year hiatus. The original Searle team had drifted apart as the aspartame project was moved to Searle's backburner when delay began to follow delay. Six months after the approval, there were 10 people in the group, including secretaries, and, most important, no sales.

There had only been $13 million in sales, primarily in Canada, up until this time. Other products would soon go to test market in 1982: General Food's adoption for Kool-Aid, and adoptions by Beatrice, Lipton, and Searle's own entry into the "tabletop" market with the newly renamed Equal brand. Searle scrambled to repackage the product in inventory, which had been written-off the books, but was fortunately very real. Ajinomoto immediately began cranking up production, as well. It had been a long, very expensive wait for Ajinomoto, and the firm must have had moments of doubt about the wisdom of teaming with Searle.

Those early days after approval are still remembered in NutraSweet. In fact, you can't forget them because one of the first applications of aspartame was in gumballs. Not a huge market, of course, but a clever marketing strategy. A mass marketing campaign was launched for *NutraSweet,* the name given aspartame, by mailing out gumballs in 1983 and then publicizing the testimonials of kids and parents who tried them. Brightly colored gumball machines containing these gumballs now stand prominently in the headquarter's hallways. These first sales proved "helpful, but certainly not life saving," as Dan Searle recounted, nor worth the 15 years of legal costs and effort expended up until then.

It was a tough sell to customers. Price was the biggest barrier, but the ongoing debates over safety in the media also made it tough for early adopters. The early professionalism of the sales effort was also questioned by some in the firm, who equated it with selling snake oil. Annette Ripper, a dietician, and Barry Homler, a researcher who would later play an important role in the R&D outreach effort, had been appearing anywhere, anytime to tell the NutraSweet story. Gradually, these and other efforts began to have an impact. It was, after all, a good tasting product which would ride the wave of diet consciousness in the largest consumer market in the world.

The FDA approval, you also need to remember, was only for "dry uses." The largest market by far for sweeteners was for "wet use" in carbonated soft drinks and juice drinks. The carbonated soft-drink market was the brass ring, with more than $25 billion in wholesale sales by 1986. The entire tabletop market for Equal, in contrast, was only $110 million in 1982. The soft-drink market had all the appearances of being mature, with essentially stable market shares and sales for the previous decade. The only segment growing by any significant measure was diet drinks. Even it had grown by only about three share points over a 15-year period. Nonetheless, within Searle there was a growing belief that aspartame could do something dramatic to this market. Call it confidence or arrogance, getting approval for wet use became the next regulatory quest for Searle.

Searle submitted a petition for wet use approval in 1982 and encountered objections which were, for the first time, explicitly addressed by the FDA when the petition was approved on July 9, 1983. This approval was welcomed because of its relative speed, but even it had its share of strange events. A number of sincere critics filed objections after the approval and were disposed of in quick succession by FDA. James Turner, who had filed the first objection with Dr. Olney in 1974, was among these, and he took the FDA's rejection to the U.S. Court of Appeals which also rejected it.

Dr. Woodrow Monte, a professor at Arizona State University, was another objector in August 1983, but, unlike the persistent Turner, he took the aspartame regulatory drama to even greater heights. In early 1984 he taped an interview for CBS that was highly critical of aspartame. Knowing that the program would be shown a few weeks later, he placed short positions on Searle stock in anticipation of what he thought would be negative investor reactions. The SEC detected the trades, notified Searle, and the story was somehow leaked to the press, including *The Wall Street Journal*.Technically, Monte did nothing illegal. What's more, he lost money because Searle stock actually rose after the interview was aired.

The sensationalism encouraged by the press was beginning to wear thin. News correspondent Dan Rather was at the height of his muckraking period and continued to focus on aspartame with a series of sensational interviews with another critic, Dick Wurtman, an MIT researcher. Wurtman was a veteran of the "MSG wars" when this food additive was being seriously questioned by critics. He had learned about the power of the media during this time, partly due to a coaching session by Ajinomoto Company, the dominant producer of MSG.

Gerry Gaull, a respected Mt. Sinai medical school pediatrician who had researched amino acids and brain damage, was hired by Searle to monitor Wurtman and the other critics. The public affairs–consumer affairs–government affairs functions were still underdeveloped within Searle because it had never had a significant presence in a mass consumption market up until then. Nor was the pharmaceutical industry very advanced in these areas at this time. Searle was beginning to catch on to what Gerry calls "the public perception of science." Searle's position had always been that science was *a self-correcting body of knowledge,* and wrong data and perception would be corrected over time. It paid, the firm felt, to be honest and upfront.

Naive? No, they still believe this, but the entry of the media into the inherent complexity and ambiguity of advanced scientific research was making it exceedingly difficult for firms to accurately communicate with the public, customers, and FDA. It was FDA Commissioner Frank Young who was quoted in the 1987 Metzenbaum hearings, which reviewed the full history of aspartame research for one final time, as saying that "science is a moving target."[3] How firms communicate about their technology and its role in producing advanced products is becoming one of today's great issues.

Wurtman was not unlike a great many researchers of this period or even today. He survived on research grants, and the pharmaceutical and food companies became important sources for support when government research grants began drying up in the 1980s. The FDA had already spent $800,000 of its own research budget in just three aspartame-related studies, a tremendous drain on the agency's small research budget of $3 million at that time. The line between objective empirical research and pressures from potential critics was becoming blurred.

On the one hand, critics demanded scientific research, but increasingly it had to be the companies themselves that had to fund the requested research. On the other hand, the validity of the data would then be questioned because they had funded the research. It was the FDA and peer reviewers in the professional research journals in which the studies were published who serve as objective arbiters. Still, critics like Wurtman could publicly demand additional studies which they would hopefully be asked to perform.

Wurtman would later play another role by assisting the National Soft Drink Manufacturers Association file its letter questioning the FDA's then pending wet use approval. This association's letter is an interesting side note in the Cola Wars, and came to play a bit part in Coke's "first strike" adoption of aspartame described in the next chapter.

It would be grossly unfair to blow off all of aspartame's critics as attention seeking, misguided researchers. They weren't. Critical researchers like Bill Pardridge at UCLA, Louis Elsas at Emory, Michael Mahalik in Philadelphia, and Jeffrey Bada at the University of California were responsible and credible critics who came forward over the years to question the impact of aspartame on consumers. Introducing a new food additive into the nation's food supply should never be easy. The system is set up to make an approval difficult, and it is kept open-ended to allow new evidence to be considered. But the question must be asked when enough proof is enough. As a consumer, I personally want that proof to be there before I place my faith in a product.

Searle and NutraSweet accept this view, yet they also believe that they had earned the right to go to market, having jumped hurdles no other company in regulatory history has ever since been asked to leap. As of now, more than 100 scientific studies have been produced establishing the safety of the product. Appendix A contains a summary of the regulatory history and the list of scientific bodies, health organizations, and governments which have approved aspartame.

By far and away the most complete review of this research, and the debate surrounding aspartame, can be found in the Congressional Record for Tuesday, November 3, 1987, which contains the report titled "NutraSweet—Health and Safety Concerns" for the Senate Committee on Labor and Human Resources.[4] This is the record of the "Metzenbaum hearings," as they were called. The scientific papers submitted for the record can quickly deaden the senses and confuse any lay reader, but the dialogue between FDA Commissioner Frank Young, Howard Metzenbaum, Bob Shapiro, and the critical researchers is captivating and unsettling. The dialogue vividly illustrates the complexity and confusion inherent in the regulatory process governing advanced technologies that impact consumers.

THE ONE-LEGGED HOPI AMENDMENT

Today, the firm puts a happy face on the whole regulatory saga by saying that this scrutiny gives them a tremendous marketing advantage. No other food additive can claim surviving that much scrutiny. The prospect of having to duplicate it with another substitute product creates a formidable entry barrier that only the largest, most committed firms would dare cross. By 1982, 13 countries would approve aspartame for use. In 1981, however, it was time to get on with building a business in anticipation of those approvals.

Kindness may be a virtue when reflecting on the experience, but everyone in Searle also acknowledges that they had shot themselves in the foot more than once. Gerry Gaull and Frank Kotsonis, NutraSweet's head of Pre-Clinical and Clinical Research, admit they were naive when it came to managing critics and the media. The law suit was ill-timed. They also underestimated how much time would be required. While they then felt they had learned from the aspartame experience, we later see with the introduction of Simplesse that one more bullet was apparently in the gun.

There was, of course, the case of the missing seven years of patent life caused by the approval stay in 1975. Remember that the firm had actually never put this product in the market, so it was seven, not six years of time lost. Mixed with the tremendous relief felt with the removal of the stay in 1981 was tremendous resentment. The patent would expire in 1986, certainly not far enough in the future to let Searle build a defensible market niche, not even enough time to recoup the investment made up to that point—approximately $100 million by some estimates. What came next was a brilliantly engineered move by Robson who effectively gave Searle the time needed to build The NutraSweet Company. It is now called by those close to its execution the "one-legged Hopi amendment." Robson simply calls it "righting a regulatory wrong."

It was Robson, himself the former head of a regulatory agency, who felt that the FDA's PBOI process had been unnecessarily long. Concerns about the data supporting aspartame's first approval had, after all, been resolved by the UAREP and FDA's own studies years earlier. During the seven years of the stay, the clock had been running on the patent, and he felt that some accommodation was called for. None was forthcoming from the normal appeal channels, so this meant finding friendly support in Congress. In 1981, the drug industry was floating an initiative called the "Patent Term Restoration Act of 1981" which called for patent extensions for some drugs under certain circumstances. Since aspartame was a food additive, its sponsors were hesitant to add aspartame to the list, but finally did so.

Roger Thies and Jim Phelps, both in Searle's legal staff at the time, had never given Robson's idea of a patent extension much hope. Once aspartame got added to the bill for consideration, they began paying more attention. Could it actually work? Roger recalls how the favorable reception at Robson's testimony on November 18, 1981, before the House Subcommittee on Courts, Civil Liberties, and the Administration of Justice finally changed his mind. In this testimony, John Robson called the FDA's handling of aspartame "an unparalleled instance of unnecessary regulatory delay and ineptitude which has worked an egregious injustice to Searle."[5] He then summarized the history of aspartame, step by painful step. Despite the warm reception given Robson, ironically this bill soon got into trouble and looked like it was heading to defeat.

It did go down, but not with aspartame in it. In a deft, last minute move, Searle's legal staff had helped move the aspartame patent extension amendment over to another bill also up for consideration, the "Orphan Drug Bill." It was added as an amendment which had seemingly general applicability to an entire set of products. The amendment was stated as applying to drugs and food additives receiving patents between such and such time, and delayed for regulatory reasons. Worded generically, to its drafters it had applicability for what they all thought was only one product—aspartame. All products fitting that description would be given an extension, but in reality the description was so restricted that it could pertain only to a single product—so called one-legged Hopi Indians. Hence the name given the amendment. This practice is common in Congress, of course, but it takes incredible attention and effort to work the process well enough to succeed.

The bill finally passed Congress in the closing hours—a real cliff-hanger. The result of Robson's long-shot idea was five and one-half more years of patent life. One-and-one-half years was considered a legitimate review time and knocked-off the seven years. As it turned out, however, there were one or two other products that managed to also fit the product description in the amendment, and their creators got an unexpected gift.

John Robson today believes that his amendment idea was the most significant contribution he was to make to NutraSweet. There is absolutely no doubt in anyone's mind that it gave the company the time it needed to experience the success that it was now about to have. This coming experience, please understand, wasn't all pleasant. Many have compared it to getting shot out of a slingshot.

CHAPTER 4

THE NEW NUTRASWEET COMPANY

There's no set game. You have to play it as it's given.
—*Ian Miller*

There were still the obvious tasks of selling the product and getting enough manufacturing capacity into place to establish the firm in the market. Six months after approval, there were no U.S. sales and only 10 people, including secretaries, formally assigned to aspartame's business development. Granted, there had probably been up to a hundred different people involved in working it through the regulatory process, but the core of dedicated, true believers who had been with it from the beginning were few in number. Regulatory attrition had exacted a toll on the original team.

To get the focus needed to bring the product to market, it was clearly time to spin aspartame out as a separate division. Division status acknowledged that aspartame was a business at last, with resource needs that dictated budgets and a specialized, adequate staff able to merchandise a food additive in a huge market. It was also a good idea to distance the product from the rest of Searle. Searle still had its own pressing needs, and its managers thought like pharmaceutical firm managers. Azarnoff, Searle's head of R&D, was already thinking about how to use aspartame's profits to fuel the rest of Searle's drug research. NutraSweet wasn't in any condition to fuel anything at that point. There surely weren't any profits to share with anyone. Searle did keep the Equal brand, however, to add a little fuel to its own research. Searle's keeping Equal also made some sense for distribution channel reasons, but the reality was that Searle's cash flows would need a boost for several years to come. Equal was given to NutraSweet only after Monsanto's acquisition in 1985.

BOB SHAPIRO GETS HIS CHANCE

The NutraSweet division was formed in 1982, just a few months after final FDA approval. The decision about who would head it is another of those unexpected and wonderfully creative events in the firm's history which seemed to become commonplace. Rumsfeld and Robson had initiated a nationwide search for the person to run the new NutraSweet Company, as it was called. Reflecting on that process, Robson recalls how unhappy he and Don were with the choices that surfaced. The "food guys" they looked at were part of an industry they didn't see as creative enough, aggressive enough, or dedicated to Searle's scientific roots. On the other hand, the "drug guys" didn't have the marketing savy needed to make a big impact in a mass market like food. Recall that the wet use petition had been filed, and its approval would mean breaking into the huge soft-drink industry.

Bob Shapiro wanted the job. That's an understatement. He wanted it badly, according to John. Bob is more modest in recounting the story. He visited Robson on two occasions to stress his strongpoints: he was an experienced attorney, could claim several years of legitimate corporate work experience, and had demonstrated creativity in restructuring some of Searle's businesses. John had also known him for 10 years. As Rumsfeld was to later comment, however, being a good lawyer doesn't guarantee that someone would also be a good businessman. Shapiro did get his message across. There's a time you have to trust intuition, and Don and John did, after all, both operate on the axiom that "bright people can do anything." Bob was bright, for sure, but neither of them could ever have expected what they would set in motion the day they announced Bob Shapiro's selection as president of The NutraSweet Company.

Shapiro's selection epitomizes one of the most fascinating features about NutraSweet. Searle had been a family-run firm facing significant challenges, and in a relatively short time had attracted surprisingly creative, aggressive leadership from notably surprising places and careers. This pattern of surprising people doing surprising things was to be repeated time and time again within NutraSweet over the next four or five years. Nutra-

Sweet was able to attract some of the most unusually creative and aggressive managers for any firm I have witnessed.

By aggressive, I mean that they persistently assert themselves and their beliefs, work insanely hard, and take risks well out of proportion to their job positions and ages. Most are young, or at least very young for the positions that they hold. What is most striking, it isn't just one or two very visible individuals—the creative mavericks idolized by Tom Peters and Robert Waterman and other management writers—but dozens of them. They were to collectively create and preserve, with pride and tremendous pleasure, a "start-up culture" driven by adrenaline and the desire to build an organization unlike any other. I talk about some of the design principles at work in their creation in Chapter 8, but this chapter tells the story about how the new company geared-up capacity from a near dead start.

Shapiro began an immediate buildup of capacity as president of the new division. During the next 12 months, the marketing function was upgraded with more people with more sophistication. The days of Annette Ripper and Barry Homler having to go around doing "dog and pony" routines for anyone who would listen were over. Olgivy & Mather, the giant advertising firm, was retained to develop marketing strategy. Ian Miller, now a senior vice president in Olgivy & Mather, was one of the early people assigned to the NutraSweet account. He literally camped out in the NutraSweet offices, and still roams the halls of corporate headquarters so much that he's considered more an employee than an outsider. Miller acknowledges that Shapiro quickly asserted himself in the marketing area in two critical ways.

The Branded Ingredient Strategy

It's a bit unclear who thought of the idea first, but Shapiro is generally given credit for the "branded ingredient" strategy. Food additives, if you read a food package label, are appetizingly listed as "monopotassium phosphate, partially hydrogenated soybean oil, FD&C Yellow 6," etc. Sugar is a known product. Consumers know what sugar is and what it does, or at least what they think it does. Aspartame has had a controversial and very visible past. It was also grouped in people's minds with saccharin and cyclamates.

NutraSweet's clients had big brand names to protect. Selling them aspartame as a replacement for sugar was going to require a massive, expensive consumer education campaign by clients and by NutraSweet. Even in 1982, Shapiro also had his eyes on 1992, and NutraSweet was going to face competition from other producers of aspartame. The perfect solution to the identity and competition problems was to give aspartame the company's name and identity. It would be NutraSweet brand aspartame, or, as it has evolved over time, simply NutraSweet.

No other food additive had used the branded ingredient strategy before. There were some analogs for other products which demonstrated how well the strategy could work. Teflon has been mentioned in the last chapter. The name *Dolby* in stereo sound systems, the successful *Cotton* label for clothing, and the *Real* label for dairy products were other examples, but there was nothing in the food industry to compare. The branded ingredient strategy was novel enough, according to Jesse Meyers, publisher of Beverage Digest, to give Bob Shapiro "a place in business history books. Not only did they (NutraSweet) make people pay through the nose for it, but they made them advertise it."[1]

Hopefully, the name NutraSweet would become synonymous with aspartame. Shapiro's position was that the company, not the client, would be the one to communicate to consumers about the safety of the product, and assuming this role was a true benefit to the customer. NutraSweet was to be positioned as a scientifically advanced, highest quality producer of food ingredients. So much so that the red and white swirl and NutraSweet name on a product would save the client the expense of communicating to their consumers about safety.

Equally important to NutraSweet, however, was the hope that it would generate automatic buyer acceptance that would make alternatives to NutraSweet unacceptable. Who makes FD&C Yellow 6? Who knows, and that is the whole point. NutraSweet's direct advertising to consumers would "pull" the aspartame through the food companies. The company spent $60 million on direct advertising in just the first three years of this strategy, and about as much in co-op advertising allowances. In contrast, total annual advertising by all artificial sweetener companies in 1981, just before aspartame's approval, had only been $3.4 million.

That, in theory, was the branded ingredient strategy. Judging from consumer awareness studies done only a couple of years after its implementation, the strategy has worked with consumers. Repeating a statistic cited previously, 98 percent of Americans can identify NutraSweet from a list as a sweetener in foods, and 70 percent can name NutraSweet unprompted as a sweetener. Whether the branded ingredient strategy is resilient enough to withstand other branded aspartame competition after 1992 is a question many inside the company and its customers are wondering these days. On the other hand, with advertising and consumer acceptance at those levels, which of the soft-drink companies wants to be the first to drop the NutraSweet logo off their cans? That is supposed to be a tough question to answer.

Redefining NutraSweet's Market

The branded ingredient strategy was important for aspartame, but Shapiro's second move was even more important for the future of the division. Shapiro saw little long-term future for the company if it defined itself only as an artificial sweetener company. Defined this narrowly, its competition became Cumberland's Sweet 'N Low, or any other artificial sweetener company that came along. NutraSweet in his mind must one day become a "high-tech food company" which would draw upon its pharmaceutical science roots to compete more broadly in the food industry. That was the future, but for the moment, aspartame was going to be much more than simply an artificial sweetener; it would become a replacement for sugar. Shapiro summarized his definition of NutraSweet's future in a *Wall Street Journal* article: "One of the cardinal rules in Western cultures is that pleasures have prices. . . . What we are saying to people is 'You can have the pleasure without paying the price.' That's like saying there is such a thing as a free lunch."[2]

Business strategists call this question of self-definition a concern about the firm's scope. By defining NutraSweet's scope broadly, the company's customers weren't just weight-conscious consumers or diabetics, but every man, woman, and child in the world. In

1981, the "every man, woman, and child" market in the United States alone represented about 2.8 billion pounds of sugar, or 80 pounds for each person, down from 102 pounds in 1972.[3] U.S. retail sales of granulated sugar accounted for $945 million and $62 million in large supermarket profits (6.6 percent of sales).

Together, sugar and high fructose corn syrup (HFCS) accounted for 99 percent of the world's consumption of carbohydrate sweeteners. The remaining 1 percent was artificial sweeteners. Hypothetically, the world market for sweeteners equated to 1.2 billion pounds of aspartame. Translated into 1985 sales, which were soon to come, a 1 percent increase in the share of this market would double NutraSweet's business.

Realistically, however, consumption of carbohydrate sweeteners in about two thirds of the world was considered either a plus or not even an issue. There aren't many fat Chinese. On the other hand, helping the People's Republic of China with a balance of trade problem caused partly by sugar imports could be more feasible. Again thinking realistically, the industrialized market was the domain for NutraSweet, and 400 million pounds of aspartame was considered the carbohydrate sweetener equivalent of the existing market size. Which market would you rather compete in: artificial sweeteners or sugar replacement? A subtle but crucial question.

The big danger in defining scope too broadly is that you can "fuzz out." You end up trying to do too many different things in too many places for the capacity you have. Sales were beginning to come in, and a number of products were in test market stages and just about ready to go. The wet use approval was still pending, and there was no way in the world that a 100 percent adoption by more than one of the soft drink companies could be satisfied with existing manufacturing capacity. In 1982 the first sales were also made in Europe using Ajinomoto production at $198 per kilo ($90 per pound). Life was beginning to dramatically speed up.

MANUFACTURING GEARS UP

The lack of manufacturing capacity wasn't unanticipated, of course. What was unanticipated was just how short capacity would be when demand took off. There was product in inventory. Remember the $21 million in inventory that was written off just before FDA's final approval? Its production costs were now nil. This stock could serve as a buffer until production could ramp-up, since Ajinomoto's capacity was grossly inadequate.

Plans had been announced in 1981 for building a large demonstration plant in University Park, just south of Chicago, using a modification of Ajinomoto technology. A major new manufacturing facility estimated at $150 million had been started next to a Searle plant in Augusta, Georgia, but it had then been stalled by the regulatory hassles. Concrete footers and rusting bolts protruded from the site. Augusta, as the plant was to be called, had been sent back to the design stage to allow for increased capacity and was again nearing ground breaking. It would be a grass roots, state of the art facility using everything NutraSweet had learned about bio-manufacturing.

The "Father of Harbor Beach"

But something very interesting had already been going on at Searle's Harbor Beach, Michigan fermentation facility. The origins of this story go back to the "Mexican barbasco root crisis" of the early 70s. Mexico was the major source of starting materials for steroid pharmaceuticals through the barbasco root, a native plant. Responding to OPEC's success, Mexico thought that it could control the steroid drug market by controlling the supply and price of barbasco root. Instead, it killed the golden goose because American buyers began developing their own fermentation technologies to produce the materials.

At the time, Searle was in the food industry in a small way through its Fermco Laboratories division which produced a line of enzyme products. Lou Goldsmith had started working for Fermco in 1971 to set up the internal manufacturing of enzymes for the food business. Harbor Beach, Michigan is about as remote a location as you can get, but Searle decided to begin producing the steroid precursor there because of an existing facility. The plant was already old and pretty run-down looking when they made modifications and started up. It had originally belonged to Hercules in the early 1960s, which would use it unsuccessfully to make MSG. It was a huge white elephant for them. Lou had managed the plant for another firm that had leased it from Hercules, and knew that it existed.

For Searle, it was a relatively smooth entry into large-scale fermentation production, and the capacity of the plant was absorbed over the first few years. As changes in technology came along, however, less and less of the plant's capacity was needed. Harbor Beach was looking very suspect as a viable operation. Drug firms are used to producing small batches of very high value product. A 2,000 gallon batch of something like they were to produce there could be worth over one-half million dollars. Harbor Beach had six 48,000 gallon fermenters! The role of excess capacity in innovation should never be ignored. The extra capacity at Harbor Beach meant that something else could also go on without disrupting normal business. It also meant that workers and management at the plant were motivated to try something else. When Searle cut back production even further, the plant management and workers had even more cause to innovate.

Goldsmith respected the Ajinomoto Company. It had already proven to be a formidable partner. Two things troubled Goldsmith in the mid-1970s, however. First, he personally wasn't convinced that the chemistry route that Ajinomoto developed and recommended was the best one for making L-phe. He believed that a fermentation process could be developed to produce this key ingredient more efficiently. The fermentation process was widely used to make amino acids, and could produce the L-isomer that was required. Several proposals to jointly develop a fermentation process were made. Ajinomoto disagreed each time, not surprisingly. Ajinomoto had invested deeply in the chemical process and understandably wanted to maintain a dominant position in the relationship.

Second, Goldsmith felt very uncomfortable having the future of the product totally in the hands of another company, particularly one which guarded information as tightly as Ajinomoto did. His concern wasn't necessarily due to the fact that Ajinomoto was a Japanese company. This was before the American paranoia of the next decade. There was clear mutual benefit for both sides in their relationship. The agreement with Ajinomoto did, however, call for them to share process technology improvement information, and that was not fast enough to satisfy some Searle scientists. Searle didn't demand access to information because of their precarious dependency upon Ajinomoto at that moment. Americans, however, don't like being controlled that way, and the independent-minded Rumsfeld and Robson especially so.

Right or wrong, creating the perception that it was not openly sharing information was a mistake for Ajinomoto. It was to make a couple of other critical errors over the next few years, but this was the one that set Lou Goldsmith off on his own quiet odyssey over the next two years. Lou went to his boss, Bob Jordt, and to Jordt's boss, Guy LaBrasse, to drum up support for a fermentation R&D project. Jordt was supportive, but the proposal was killed at higher levels. The response was "Let's think about it." Keep in mind the status of aspartame at that time. The UAREP and PBOI studies were crawling along, and their outcomes were far from certain. Lukewarm would be an optimistic assessment of the response to Lou's idea among the higher-ups within Searle.

Lou was a corporate scientist. He had scientific curiosity balanced with respect for management authority. What finally sent Lou Goldsmith over the line, however, were his increasing contacts with Ajinomoto, particularly his first trip to Japan in January 1979. He discovered that Ajinomoto had been working on a fermentation approach for five years. Ajinomoto researchers claimed that their work confirmed that the fermentation process was still too expensive and not very efficient in terms of yield. Lou couldn't believe it, and asked to study the data. Still not convinced, he returned to Searle and with Jordt's support immediately began bootlegging research funds for his own test. They chose to take their superiors' neutral response as neither an approval nor disapproval. That, in their minds, was enough for a go ahead.

Harbor Beach enters the scene here because it was already doing fermentation process production and development. Lou hired a young Ph.D. microbiologist, Ron Myers, to run his bootlegged project. A small workspace in the Harbor Beach labs was garnered. The first step was selecting a suitable culture, the very foundation of the fermentation process, for development and improvement.

The world of microbiology and fermentation technology had already advanced considerably during the 1970s. Fermentation had been one of the world's earliest means for altering food. Several early civilizations, notably the Phoenician, had been making a variety of alcoholic drinks, with beer and wine heading the list. Over time, the technology improved as we improved the quality of the microbes used and better controlled the fermentation environment.

Doing fermentation is one thing, but doing it with maximum quality control and commercial efficiency is something else entirely. It is not easy. It is possible to improve the quality of the end product and the amount produced from a given batch only by gradually improving the microbial strain and managing the governing conditions in which they work on their source materials, which are usually agricultural carbohydrates. It is laborious, painstaking, continuous work to gradually improve a microbe strain through either mutation or selection. In a given fermentation process, for example one batch yields significantly more end product than others. Those cultures are saved and the conditions are noted—duration, temperature, agitation. The cultures are used again, varying conditions to see if other even better strains emerge from that iteration. It may be that a bottleneck is encountered in the process because the microbes, which are sometimes called "bugs," haven't "learned" how to move from one step to another. Over successive iterations of the process, some do make that move efficiently, and they are isolated and used again.

Genetic engineering has recently altered this trial-and-error, time-consuming approach to fermentation technology. Bio-engineering using recombinant technologies is becoming increasingly common. High fructose corn syrup producers use such technology, for example, to speed up and improve the efficiency of the process. French champagne producers have also introduced bio-engineered yeast into their production process to speed up the *rèmuage* process stage, thus saving almost three months.[4] These applications are not only safe but don't affect flavor since the organisms never leave a controlled environment and never become part of the end product. An entirely new strain is not created. The applications make it possible to leapfrog ahead to create a strain with the needed qualities. It speeds up the "training" cycle and gets the firm to the most efficient solution quicker.

Once a solution is arrived at which hits a goal of so many grams per liter, then it's on to commercial scale. Process information is guarded as much as possible since it represents tremendous competitive advantage. The process can also be patented. There is a "library" of patented microbial cultures which a firm can draw upon to shorten its own experimentation stage. In 1979, bio-engineering was still in its infancy. Doing it the hard way from scratch by gradually improving a strain was possible but also unrealistic. Goldsmith and Myers decided to use one of the cultures in the library, even though it had very low productivity.

In only 10 months, Ron Myers and one assistant reached 50 percent of the project's goal. They had a patentable process, but not a commercial one. By mid-1980, only 18 months from its start, they reached that goal. Lou's job had changed in the interim, and he was now working more closely with Ajinomoto. Searle's attitude had also changed. There were now even fewer qualms about asking for information from Ajinomoto. The "special relationship," while still solid, was being more actively managed on the Searle side.

Up to this point, Lou had been given access to Ajinomoto's fermentation-process data, but not their cultures. Ajinomoto was asked, and finally agreed, to provide a sample to compare with the Harbor Beach culture. The Ajinomoto culture was still superior, but not enough so that Searle wanted to adopt it. The culture comparison was all the proof they needed. Lou's little enterprise was given official status and a budget to quickly take the bootlegged L-phe process up to full production scale. This they did, and Searle was soon in control of its own proprietary culture and process technology to make the most complex and costly component for aspartame. The majority of the process to produce aspartame remained Ajinomoto's, however.

Ajinomoto questioned Searle's ability to produce a better strain. Industry observers also couldn't believe that Searle had, or would even have tried to develop, its own culture and process. There were several erroneous press statements during this time which drew no responses from Searle. Searle was content to not say anything to dispel those inaccurate perceptions for competitive reasons. The company remembered how close a foot race it had been to get the use patent in the first place. Contractually, Searle had to share information with Ajinomoto only about improvements to Ajinomoto's own original technology. Now, the proverbial shoe was put on the other foot.

The debate over which part of which technology was or was not used in various aspartame-related processes would heat up and sometimes strain the two partners' relationship over the following years. The Ajinomoto position remained firm and clear. The regulatory process had been both extremely uncomfortable and expensive for them, and yet they had remained dedicated to the relationship. It would be fair to guess that Ajinomoto's management would wonder whether they had made a good choice in joining with Searle. Its leadership could now also legitimately ask whether Searle was dealing openly and sincerely. A more cautious, respectful, and much more evenly balanced relationship came to prevail. Even more so after the Monsanto acquisition.

Still, Ajinomoto must surely regret their earlier decisions to avoid joint fermentation development and to hold back their cultures until Searle had developed their own. The importance of these decisions would be driven home for Ajinomoto again in 1988 when NutraSweet would actually sell L-phe back to Ajinomoto at a lower cost than Ajinomoto could apparently make it. This was a very, very sweet psychic victory for many on the manufacturing side of NutraSweet. The general Japanese unwillingness to openly share information with their foreign business partners continues to haunt them even today.

The Harbor Beach success was important for another reason than the realigning of power in the Ajinomoto-Searle relationship. Searle would remain partially dependent upon Ajinomoto process technology for many more years. Very importantly, Harbor Beach had also shown Searle that it could manufacture, not just buy, extremely complex components for aspartame.

Some finance people never totally bought into the idea of self-manufacturing, but they could at least now be convinced to go along with the manufacturing buildup that was soon to occur.

Lou Goldsmith's willingness to take risks we now call *intrapreneuring,* and this little saga needs to be added to the list of other notable internal venturing successes within American corporations.[5] Most important, it is an early demonstration that a one-sided relationship with a Japanese partner can be rebalanced.

It would be very unfair to blame Ajinomoto for consciously trying to control Searle. Shortly after Bob Shapiro became president, he became concerned about the status of the Searle-Ajinomoto relationship. Max Downham was asked in 1982 to investigate what had contributed to its "rocky" status, and Max had to conclude that Searle had probably not completely kept the spirit of the initial relationship. The FDA inquiry had frustrated Ajinomoto, and the delay had been used by Searle, it appeared to Ajinomoto management, to improve Searle's position. Ajinomoto had gone from being the sole-producer to only being a cross-licensee.

Gearing Up at University Park and Harbor Beach

Still, Ajinomoto remained indispensable to NutraSweet. Manufacturing plans and activity would dramatically escalate from 1981 on, and working with at least one known process technology helped. Hundreds of millions of dollars would be invested in manufacturing over the next few years, and much of this sum would have to be committed before final beverage approval was even in sight. The very first U.S. aspartame plant needed to be built, and it would use Ajinomoto's tested process. There's nothing like investing in a known quantity when time is so short.

Back in the 1960s, HUD had tried building model urban development projects on the south side of Chicago with mixed success. An important component of these projects was supposed to be industrial parks that would attract firms that would hopefully generate jobs. The Park Forest South–University Park area was one of these projects. In early fall 1981, Searle leased space in a building previously occupied by a pharmaceutical firm that had gone out of business. University Park was meant to be a demonstration project to learn how to produce aspartame, but it soon came to assume a critical supply role when demand took-off beyond expectations.

John Grove, who would become the first University Park manager, tells a great story about those first days and months. Grove was working for Rhom & Haas when he read about the FDA approval in *Chemical Week*. Shortly after that he was contacted by a search firm and told the first start-up would either be Augusta or Ireland. He soon found out that a demonstration plant would be built at University Park and joined the start-up team. It would be fun, he thought, and the future of the product sounded bright. John was to find, like so many others who were joining up at the same time, that he would get more than he bargained for. He would be joining a classic "skunk works" of the first order.

The key to success at University Park, according to Grove, would be to bring capacity on-line as demand grew. Searle was still very skittish about investing in large-scale manufacturing ventures of any kind. Seeing the sale in hand would make spending the money easier. The decision had also been made to be "wasteful," that is, not try to immediately achieve the lowest costs, but to spend the money to build inventory and learn as much as possible. Grove even recounts how Gary Whitehouse, then vice president for manufacturing, would understate investment requirements to get the financial guys to buy into the project. Risky for careers, but his strategy worked. The total investment would eventually be four times the initial forecast.

The trade-off that was made by gradually starting-up and adding capacity as needed was that the efficiency of the overall production process at the end of the buildup could be less than that of a large-scale, single-stage start-up. This would actually later prove to be true, but the benefits were to show up in other nice ways, as well. University Park's team had the time to learn, twink, and improve Ajinomoto's initial technology. The gradual learning and experimentation would allow Grove and the other team members to up production in 1984 by 40 percent over what the plant's capacity was supposed to be. Those levels of increases aren't uncommon in NutraSweet, but the timing of this one was particularly welcomed.

Those kinds of results also illustrate my point about the people then pouring into NutraSweet, not just in manufacturing but in marketing and research as well. Their training and backgrounds were incredibly varied, but they shared many other qualities. In their eyes, nothing was a "given," everything was up for grabs, and the present status of something simply represented one more opportunity to see how the next outcome could be different, hopefully better than the last. Their open challenging and experimenting with parameters and limits originated from the very heart of the organization—Rumsfeld and Robson in Searle, with Dan Searle as cheerleader, and Shapiro in NutraSweet.

Over the next few years, Shapiro and Downham would work hard at articulating the NutraSweet culture, yet this unique quality of mind would escape capture in words. It was almost a physical reaction I observed during my travels around the company, particularly in the plants. Mention the word "new" and "challenge" in the same sentence, and a glaze would appear in the eyes of the person you were talking to. Without having to say more, their response would be "When?"

While so critical to success initially, the "start-up mentality" that was nurtured during that time has today come to pose a challenge to the cohesiveness of NutraSweet's company culture. As the aspartame business moves closer to a low-cost producer position in NutraSweet's business strategy matrix, a clash of old and new cultures may be inevitable. Whether a "start-up culture" can ever be compatible with the structure and routine inherent in a "low-cost producer" culture is a good question. The one emphasizes experimentation, initiative, and autonomy while the other stresses planning, risk avoidance, and active involvement from top management. Other firms appear to have made the transition, some better, others worse, as later chapters note.

The start-up culture was fortunately alive and well at University Park, Harbor Beach, and Augusta. That surprising 40 percent capacity increase at University Park was warmly welcomed because wet use approval had come in the interim. Adoptions by the soft-drink companies were threatening to overwhelm capacity, and it was not inconceivable that one of them could even capture enough aspartame production to effectively control their own diet soft-drink markets. The thought had once even crossed PepsiCo's Roger Enrico's mind. With the additional production coming when it did at University Park, the possibility of any one customer ever controlling production was defeated.

Meanwhile, the small experimental project at Harbor Beach had turned the place upside down—or inside out, to be more accurate. Harbor Beach, it was decided, would become the primary source of L-phe. Radical modifications were first needed. Huge processing vessels and other equipment were literally scrounged from wherever they could be found, retrofitted, and put into place as quickly as possible. Little of this equipment was brand new due to the long time lags involved in buying new equipment. As a result, Harbor Beach was up and running with the proprietary Searle L-phe process in less than half the time it would have taken to build a new plant from scratch.

But most of the building was old and certainly not large enough to accommodate much further capacity. What came next was one more in an increasingly long string of creative decisions. A much larger, new building was designed and built around the old existing frame building. Once in place, the older building, now completely contained within the new one, was taken down without ever ceasing production. New equipment was introduced in stages until the entire plant was new. Today, Harbor Beach is one of the most efficient NutraSweet operations, and the memories of the old early days are contained mostly in Lou Goldsmith's photo albums.

Augusta Cranks Up

Many industry observers today think that NutraSweet's Augusta plant was built to be close to one of the company's major customers, Coca-Cola Company in Atlanta. The location does help in many respects, but the actual truth, according to some wags, is that Dan Searle, a passionate golfer, wanted to be close to Augusta's famous golf courses. Perhaps more accurately, Searle already had a plant in Augusta, and the land was already permitted and accessible. The fact that Coca-Cola, the site, and the golf courses were also near at hand added to the site's attractiveness.

The city of Augusta is an anachronism, like so much of the new South. Sitting on the Savannah River in the Piedmont region of the Georgia-South Carolina border, Augusta had escaped the ravages of the Civil War, as many of the old, restored antebellum houses stand witness. It was the South of magnolias, wealthy family dynasties, well-defined social order, rich farm land, and grinding rural poverty. Once each year the city graciously hosts the Masters' Golf Tournament, one of the world's truly big-money golfing events. Tickets are practically passed down from generation to generation, and the city glows in spring flowers.

Life speeded-up when the Savannah River Project facility opened across the river in the late 1940s. The plant produces nuclear-weapons-grade materials, and has since become a major hazardous waste threat to the entire region. But when it started up, Savannah River began hiring hundreds of skilled employees and technical staff, many from outside the South. A few chemical companies had also located in Augusta, including Searle which produced pharmaceutical chemicals. Collectively, the heavy, rapid investment by these companies had created a boom economy for Augusta which was transforming the city and region. This same process was being replicated throughout the South.

Along with the prosperity came an occasionally off-color morning sky from the chemical vapors flowing from the tall stacks to the southeast of the city. One of the great ironies about the Searle site was its neighboring firm, Columbia Nitrogen. This plant was owned by Dutch State Mines, one of the two joint venture parents of Holland Sweetener, which would become years later one of NutraSweet's aspartame competitors in Europe and Canada. Small world, indeed.

The FDA stay had killed the first attempted construction of the new plant. The concrete foundation and rusting steel footings stood witness over those years to the frustrating regulatory process. So much was being learned at Harbor Beach and University Park, however, that the original Augusta plans needed to be scrapped anyway. A much larger facility was planned, and a new foundation poured as the regulatory process began to show signs of progress. Augusta would produce both L-phe and finished product, APM as it is called, in two different manufacturing groups within the same site.

The second plant design would initially utilize the same Ajinomoto process used at University Park to speed the start-up, but the plant was to be designed to accommodate subsequent improvements which were already being explored. The Harbor Beach experience was already helping other parts of the company. Dan Searle, Rumsfeld, and Robson had bitten the bullet and committed the needed funds. Ajinomoto had not been given an opportunity to co-invest in Augusta. As a consequence, Ajinomoto's financial returns and access to new technology from Augusta's development would diminish over time as NutraSweet's own proprietary process technology was introduced at Augusta. NutraSweet was learning.

With the removal of the FDA stay, and the unexpected approval of the wet use petition, it was "run and gun" time at Augusta. Steel structures were going up at the same time employees were coming on board. The first employees came over from the Searle plant. Those employees were given a choice to either stay or come over to the new plant—not an easy choice since it meant trading Searle's security for the uncertainty of a new product still in the market development. Those who made the move tended to be the younger, more ambitious workers who saw a limited future on the Searle side.

The Searle plant's loss of its talented people created bitter feelings between the two plants for some time, and minor sniping continued across the fence for months. Bobby Mims, who was working inside the Searle plant and would eventually become the new NutraSweet plant's controller, had to find out about a job opening in the local newspaper. The two plants now live in even more different worlds, and those who had voted with their feet to join NutraSweet feel they made the right choice.

Other staff joined in response to recruiters and ads running in papers throughout the manufacturing Southeast. Dave Sharp, who would one day come to run one of the units at

Augusta, would be one of these. Dave had been working for Monsanto in Nitro, West Virginia and for another chemical company before chucking it for the risk of a new start-up. Paul Givens was another of the early sign-ups, and he, along with Mims and the other early managers, soon became part of an emerging pattern. Givens, for example, had boundless energy and a Ph.D. in Chemistry. He, like so many of the others, would wear a hard hat and jeans, run on adrenaline and caffeine for 12-to-14 hours a day for weeks at a time, constantly prowling around the site looking for problems to attack. By April 1984, a year after wet use approval eventually came, many of them were founding members of the "Gang of 54" managers and technical staff that had signed-up.

Pirate Flag over Augusta?

Without exception, the members of this group were young—much younger than most of the line workers and hourly employees also being hired. The average age of the management group was likely in the mid-30s. The place was awash with talent, even at the line operator levels. NutraSweet had been hiring former firemen, teachers, anyone willing to do something new. Often they were hired the day they were interviewed—"Yeah, sounds good. So, when can you start?" While snap judgments were being made, a positive attitude and willingness to dive into an unstructured situation were attributes uniformly being screened for. The interviewing process was in the hands of the managers needing the people.

These lower level employees would be given an intensive training session and then placed into positions which they were then asked to improve. Formal programs like "total quality control" were not installed until years later; at that time it simply seemed logical to ask the folks doing the jobs to find and implement ways to improve them. There was no historical baggage nor old sages around Augusta to tell someone how things had always been done in the past—"There were no blueprints for this organization," as one manager put it. They had to create and live with their own standards and criteria, except for two totally binding ones: quality and safety came first, low cost second. Remember that NutraSweet was part of a pharmaceutical firm, with pharmaceutical industry standards. Their manufacturing facilities were totally unlike those found in the rest of the chemical and food industries at that time. Infusing those high standards into the new plant was a continuous task.

The original gang members were also often from "outside the South"—Yankees, to be quite honest—still without their families at that point. Call it team building, but the members did a lot of intense bonding at numerous "fraternity parties." The work climate was intentionally informal, and kept much like that of a family. They all had had it with frigid, big company cultures, and they were not taking the career risks associated with a new plant start-up only to end up recreating the very conditions they had fled. Problems and hassles were worked out on the spot, often in "boardwalk meetings" that took place on the wooden boardwalk connecting the ugly 40-foot brown trailers surrounded by Georgia clay and a maze of steel.

Jim McDermott, the first plant manager at Augusta, reinforced the emerging maverick culture. He was somewhat "laid back" in terms of style—as long as construction was ahead of schedule and people were working as hard as they could. Appearance was secondary. Ralph Bietz was an interesting case in point. Ralph's microbiology background and experience in seven previous plant start-ups for other firms made him invaluable as head of the L-phe unit. He was in his early 30s when he joined NutraSweet, but photos of Ralph from those early days reveal long hair sticking out from under his hard hat.

When Jim McDermott left shortly after Augusta's start-up, it was Ralph who was picked to replace him. For a while he kept his long hair, but finally cut it back (not off), and even conceded to such stringent norms as neckties for managers when visitors were in town. Ralph, like so many of the others, was bright, energetic, assertive, and could capture people's commitment. He was most comfortable wearing his hard hat, out in the plant. Typical of the prevailing management style was his saying, "Don't make decisions to make you look good. Make them to make the plant look good."

The intense pressures of compressed deadlines, high quality standards, geographical distance from Deerfield, a strong sense of a close community in a strange new location, and the personal commitment to the new plant's success were all forces working together to forge an unusually strong culture. To outsiders, the Augusta plant's personnel came to appear cocky, even arrogant and "irreverent." Because Augusta was so important to NutraSweet, the plant was getting whatever money and staff it needed. Whether the employees were prima donnas or not was a question of where you stood. Were they perhaps just overly proud? They could never be criticized for not being team players. As one Augusta manager put it when talking about the early need to modify Ajinomoto's process, "What we did was the equivalent of turning a motorcycle into an eight-cylinder Lincoln."

Through some marginally controlled and then little understood process, the Augusta plant emerged with its own unique cultural chemistry. It was effective to the extreme in terms of getting the plant up and running. Augusta was the model and pace-setter for the firm. It always produced the most at least cost, etc., etc. The "Augusta story" was getting monotonous to a few people at headquarters and the other plants. Still, Augusta deserves to be recognized for the exceptional creation it was, and needed to be, at that critical time.

But similar stories could also be told about the other plants, as well. It's just that Augusta was so colorful! Take the story of the pirate flag, for example. Ralph came to work one morning to discover the planned raising of a pirate flag over the building. There had been half-joking, half-serious discussions among gang members for some time about raising the flag. Had the mavericks gone so far as to become pirates within the company?

Closer inspection of the situation revealed that it wasn't just any old pirate flag. It was the flag of the Oakland Raiders, whose owner, Al Davis, had created the team motto, "A Commitment to Excellence." The Raiders played a rough game, looked like hell, got into trouble, but they also won games. Granted, the motto was right for Augusta, but raising the black pirate/Oakland Raider flag had to be reconsidered, Ralph suggested. It never did fly, but it never really had to.

There is, to be sure, a dark side to strong group cultures. They can cut both ways. On the one hand, Augusta did the near impossible in terms of executing a high quality, from scratch, start-up using a new work force. On the other hand, "start-up cultures" can become overly risky when a plant has to de-emphasize autonomous experimentation by one group which should actively collaborate with other groups in the company. Once the plant eventually goes into full swing, and the goal becomes one of cost minimization with maximum production, the rules must also change to some extent. What happens to the earlier successful start-up culture? Can it, must it, also change?

Not only was the initial process modified and implemented, but a new hybrid process was introduced and implemented in 1987. But the new process came on-line much harder, due to its complexity. The complexity of the newer technologies painfully demonstrated to everyone in Augusta the need for very active communication, collaboration, and a team approach which extended well beyond Augusta. The cultural gulf between Deerfield and Augusta had been deepening as a "them versus us" feeling crept into the relationship between the plant and corporate levels. A few plant managers even came to refer jokingly, but cynically to themselves as "plant life."

This split was the fault of both plant and corporate management, and was certainly not what anyone ever wanted. It was all too common in other companies, and if there was one thing that NutraSweet wanted more than anything else, it was to be better, to be different than everyone else. Bob Shapiro and Max Downham were working hard at developing and communicating an overall NutraSweet culture in an attempt to find the glue to hold together all the parts of the very gangly, rapidly growing company. (This culture was finally manifested in the mission statement in Appendix B.)

While such efforts were critical to unifying the parts of a new company, it is a tough job, to say the least. Personally, I'm not convinced that it is ever a good idea to abandon a start-up culture. Toning it down, and redirecting it to other challenges such as continuous quality improvement, are desirable options. In a dynamic market, the values personified in a start-up environment must have a lasting place. Finding the right balance is the trick.

This point was demonstrated in late 1989 when it was announced that Monsanto was springing for a major capacity expansion in Augusta in preparation for 1992. The message to competitors was meant to be clear: NutraSweet and Monsanto are in the aspartame business for keeps. Capacity would nearly double, and the challenges of doing this while still keeping production up were going to be formidable. The lessons about collaboration had been learned—no talk about pirate flags this time. One of the convincing factors in the decision to do the expansion in Augusta rather than another site was surely the gleam in the eyes of the Augusta managers when the possibility first surfaced. I was poking around Augusta at the time, and watched the anxiety level climb until Monsanto's decision was announced. As Dave Sharp put it upon hearing the news, "Great. Let's go start digging dirt." Ahhh, adrenaline. . . .

CHAPTER 5

INTO THE COLA WARS

They're all lawyers! They don't know
anything about customer management or the
soft drink business; without this patent
they couldn't sell their way out of a
paper bag.[1]
—*Roger Enrico*

Enrico's quote from his book done with Jesse Kornbluth, *The Other Guy Blinked: How Pepsi Won the Cola Wars,* neatly summarizes the feelings of more than one food company executive about NutraSweet from 1982 to 1984. The simple truth was that few experienced, marketing-strategy people existed in Searle, let alone NutraSweet, during this time period. Selling drugs was one thing. Selling to the food industry giants—which had practically created modern advertising and mass marketing—was going to be something else. Before NutraSweet had finished shouldering its way into their markets, the company would antagonize many of those executives and earn a reputation from its competitors for aggressive marketing. What NutraSweet simply did was question the norms and assumptions which had come to prevail over many decades in those markets.

Aspartame in Kool-Aid was nice, but the young company's future depended on its ability to penetrate the huge soft-drink market. In what was starting to become a familiar pattern to outside company observers, Shapiro turned his company's disadvantage upside down. He actually viewed the lack of food industry experience not so much as a liability but as an opportunity to totally rethink the marketing and pricing of their only product. If that meant violating some industry taboos and practices, so be it. NutraSweet would do the same thing with Simplesse, as the next chapter points out. He approached the task of marketing aspartame with the mental mindset of a lawyer with a good, tight, but untested case.

The facts of the case were there. Aspartame had endured a costly regulatory process and survived as the most heavily researched "safe" food additive in history. The hurdle had been set high for anyone wanting to follow their path with a competing product. Dry use applications by Beatrice Companies, Nestlé, and General Foods were demonstrating aspartame's great taste. The company knew that taste tests had already been quietly done by Coca-Cola and PepsiCo which confirmed aspartame's exceptional compatibility with their diet formulations. The stuff tasted as good as sugar. These companies were getting aspartame for their tests in Japan and Canada where aspartame was already approved for wet use. Saccharin had just been smashed in the press and was only allowed in the market because nothing else was there. The advertising of the NutraSweet brand name directly to consumers, bypassing the companies, was also creating demand. And, best of all, NutraSweet had a use patent with an extended life to 1992.

Don Rumsfeld thought that these basic advantages were so strong that he would one day give Shapiro a large stuffed monkey for his office to symbolize how "Even a monkey could sell the stuff." That incident quickly got around the company, somewhat to Rumsfeld's discredit, but it illustrated how pleased, even envious, the rest of Searle was with NutraSweet's strong position.

So what would you do in such an attractive competitive position? Right. Price as high as the market could bear, and produce as much as you possibly could. There were a few complications to this scenario. First, production wasn't going to come on-line as quickly as needed to satisfy all customers. Shortages were inevitable until Augusta came on-line late in 1984 or 1985. In fact, a few customers were upset with the company because it was using direct advertising at a time when the product was in short supply. Either marketing was not in touch with manufacturing, or the company was trying to get demand, and price, as high as possible. Second, no one really knew how to price the stuff. How high could you go? What's worse, if you priced too low, you'd leave money on the table which would be lost forever. The soft-drink giants had also found that a blend of saccharin and aspartame was easily possible, and certainly desirable from a cost standpoint. It was clear that aspartame would change the economics of the soft-drink companies, as Table 5–1 illustrates.

Saccharin was clearly a gold mine for the soft drink companies, given the fact that a can of saccharin-sweetened soft drink sold at the same price as a can of their sugared product. In 1982, Coca-Cola had engineered a glitsy Radio City Music Hall roll-out for Diet Coke, the first new brand to which it attached the company's own name. Diet Coke was formulated with saccharin, and now putting health warning labels on millions of cans bearing this American institution's name wasn't a happy prospect.

Despite its successful taste tests and solution to the prospect of saccharin warning labels, aspartame was seen as a great unknown, if not a threat, by PepsiCo and Coca-Cola. It had the potential for upsetting the carefully waged competitive struggle between these two giants. Smaller companies like Royal Crown and Dr Pepper were much more receptive, since aspartame was one more tool to pry market share from the two big firms. But aspartame would be very expensive for them, also. It was safe to say that there could be some "buyer resistance."

NutraSweet did encounter some resistance; that is perhaps a gross understatement. The soft drink firms practically choked

TABLE 5–1
Price per Equivalent Sweeteners for Various Sweeteners for Soft Drinks—1985

Sweetener	Approximate 1985 Price per Pound	Relative Sweeteners Index	Price Relative to Sugar (per use)
Sugar	0.27	1	0.27
High fructose corn syrup	0.20	1	0.20
Saccharin	2.90	300	0.01
Aspartame	90.00	180	0.54

Source: NutraSweet Company.

when they first heard Shapiro's terms. NutraSweet's experience in entering a new large market is a lesson for any young firm with a product to sell in a tough market dominated by a few large firms. Shapiro and his crew of young managers were wading into one of the most hotly contested markets then in existence—the blood feud that had already been raging for two decades called "the cola wars."

A BRIEF HISTORY OF THE COLA WARS

Flavored soft drinks have been popular for more than a hundred years in the United States. Coca-Cola was introduced in Georgia in 1886 and Pepsi-Cola in North Carolina in 1898. Dr Pepper had beaten them both into the market, being introduced in 1885. All three originated in the South where "soda jerks" working behind counters in local pharmacies would routinely experiment with different concoctions.

From these beginnings per capita consumption has increased at an annual rate of about 6 percent: from .6 gallons in 1889 to 3.3 gallons in 1929, 23.4 gallons in 1969, and 44.5 gallons in 1985.[2] Consumption was down in 1988 to an average annual increase of 4.5 percent. This average is deceptive since the increase is 3.2 percent for sugared product and 8.4 percent for diet product![3] To put these figures in perspective, enough Coca-Cola alone has been consumed, according to 1987 company statistics, that if poured over Niagara Falls it would flow at a normal rate for 23 hours and 21 minutes, or circle the earth in cans laid end-to-end 429 times.[4] Today, the soft drink market is valued at nearly $27 billion wholesale and more than $43 billion at retail.[5]

The soft-drink market is huge, for sure, and worth competing in for just for that reason. It is becoming much more of a global market as well. The Coca-Cola Company, for example, views foreign markets as its major source of future growth. It made more money in foreign markets in 1989 than it did in the United States.

But competition in the soft-drink market is also very much a personal thing. This is true for both the companies and the consumers of their products. Without a doubt, the advertising themes with which these firms battle each other have made deep impressions on people: Pepsi's "Pepsi Generation" and Coke's 1971 classic, updated in 1990, "I'd Like to Buy the World a Coke," as examples. In reality, it appears that consumers routinely switch between major soft drinks based on their availability and price. Still, the ability of these firms and their advertising agencies to wrap catchy themes around prevailing social trends is unique in consumer marketing. As Steve Ste. Marie, a former manager of channel marketing for PepsiCo, pointed out in a conversation:

> In the mid-1960s, Pepsi-Cola and their advertising agency, BBDO, devised an advertising strategy aimed at clearly differentiating Pepsi and Coke in the mind of the consumer; their conclusion: avoid the product-driven orientation of competition and elevate the perceived social value of the Pepsi brand. The creation of the Pepsi generation established a new creative platform—the consumer is the hero and the product, in this case Pepsi, symbolizes a lifestyle, one which all of us could share. This marketing philosophy was the first step in redefining marketing strategy for the soft drink category. Pepsi championed a "run and shoot" style of event-driven marketing as contrasted to the more conservative "blocking and tackling" approach of other package goods companies.

Consumers may see Michael Jackson or George Michael on their TVs pitching one or the other of these soft drinks, but what they would never fully appreciate is the very serious pitched battle between these companies for each 10th of a point in market share. No other competition is followed so closely that changes in share points are routinely and broadly reported by the major media. The combat is so intense that the names of their arch rival would reportedly not be mentioned in either corporate headquarters.

As Figure 5–1 illustrates, competition can occur in several distribution channels, with one or the other companies holding dominant position in one channel or another. Pepsi may outsell Coke in grocery stores, but Coke's control over vending and fountain food service channels is so strong that Pepsi still trails in overall market share.

Coca-Cola's relative share of the total market used to be much greater: 32.6 percent for all brands versus 20.5 percent for Pepsi in 1973, for example. Seven-Up, Dr Pepper, Royal Crown,

FIGURE 5–1
Soft Drink Industry Channels

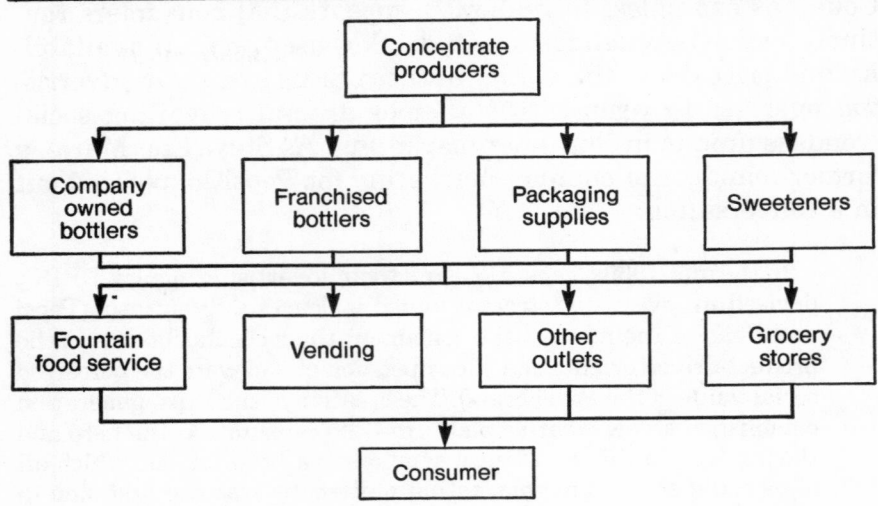

and any other producer held the difference. By 1986, however, Coca-Cola had gained share to 39.8 percent while Pepsi-Cola had moved to 30.6 percent. The other companies had all lost share.[6]

Most recently, Pepsi lost a few tenths of a point against Coca-Cola, but the time period of greatest interest to us preceded 1983. Up until this year, the Cola Wars had gone through several major stages. Pepsi kicked them off around 1933 by selling 12-ounce bottles for the same price as Coca-Cola's 6½-ounce bottles. Pepsi gained a lasting place in the market due to Coke's slow response, but Coke still held such a dominant lead that Pepsi managers developed an acute underdog image over the years. They would always be a distant second unless something fundamentally different occurred—which it did in the 1960s.

Competition began shifting from packaging and pricing strategies to "lifestyle marketing" in the 1960s. In 1962 Royal Crown Cola Co. introduced Diet Rite, which tasted great and became a big seller until the Coca-Cola Company introduced Tab in 1963 and PepsiCo introduced Diet Pepsi in 1964. The diet brands were astutely introduced at the beginning of the health and dieting wave which was beginning in the United States. No one could gauge the duration and scale of this wave.

The marketing guys in Pepsi were the first to really understand the implications of lifestyle marketing, although they also made an occasional mistake in tapping the sentiment of consumers. Don Kendall had become CEO of PepsiCo, and he began infusing a new aggressive spirit into the company. The Pepsi managers he inducted into the war were younger and given tremendous autonomy in experimenting with marketing and distribution strategies. Some of his later management choices like Larry Higby, Roger Enrico, and John Sculley were examples of the talent to be drafted. The 1963 "Pepsi Generation" campaign hit the mark so squarely that Pepsi narrowed Coke's lead to a 2-to-1 margin, compared to a 5-to-1 margin, by the end of the 1970s.[7] In the eyes of Pepsi executives, Coca-Cola appeared tired and most willing to defend share, not attack.

Complicating the war was the 1970 banning of cyclamate. Saccharin was the only artificial sweetener available, but it tasted terrible. Pepsi shot itself in the foot by trying to counter the bad taste with a saccharin/sugar blend while Tab switched to a 100 percent saccharin formula. Taste wasn't what consumers wanted, Pepsi soon found in taste tests. Consumers wanted the one calorie. By the time Pepsi switched to 100 percent saccharin and a diet-oriented campaign, Tab had secured a solid 2-to-1 sales margin in a market segment that most industry experts conceded to be the future of the industry.

The battles got bloodier from this point on. The "Pepsi Challenge" in 1975 was their first head-on collision in public. The blind taste tests run by Pepsi had shown consumers preferring Pepsi to Coke, and Pepsi then blitzed the media with these claims. A good percentage of Pepsi's bottlers wouldn't run the ads because they were so aggressive and invited retaliation. Coke did counter with rebates and rival claims, but the damage was already done. Pepsi passed Coke in food store sales for the first time with a 1.4 share point lead in 1979.

Turnabout is fair play, as the saying goes. The head-on comparison between brands as a strategy would later haunt Pepsi in 1989 when Coca-Cola would attack Pepsi's sugar-based product with Diet Coke. That was an unusual, incredibly creative strategy, industry observers noted, but whether Diet Coke could surpass the Pepsi brand was less certain. Still, it was a real statement about the trend toward products for the health conscious consumer. It also reflected the creative and aggressive new culture taking hold within the Coca-Cola Company during the 1980s.

In 1980 Coca-Cola experienced its own management revolution when Robert Goizueta became CEO and Don Keough president. Only a year earlier, Brian Dyson had been made president of Coca-Cola USA. Dyson had been given a mandate to shake up the division, and Keough and Goizueta were thinking the same way. Coke went on the offense. Several swift, gigantic moves followed, which gave testimony that Coke was first, and going to stay first, in this market.

One of the first moves was to cut costs by adopting lower cost high fructose corn syrup. Changing the taste of the flagship brand was unexpected and bold. HFCS allowed Coke to cut prices which Pepsi couldn't fully match for some time. While not completely successful in recouping retail share loss, by 1983 the move had helped Coke. Consumers were gradually weaned from sugar by increasing HFCS and cutting sugar content during this time period. The price competition has had lasting impact; discounting has become an industry norm.

The smaller companies were not completely on the sideline. Royal Crown Cola had a good tasting product, and had also shown a willingness to innovate and attack the larger companies. It was the first company to introduce a "caffeine-free" product. The Seven-Up Co., of course, was able to make the same claim, and these two companies soon attracted the attention of Coca-Cola and Pepsi which countered with their own versions. While consumers may switch brands of caffeine-free soft drinks, the barrage of advertising was shaping consumer behavior; consumers were becoming even more diet and health conscious. The companies were now amplifying the trend.

Unfortunately for the smaller firms, in the 1980s they were shuffled from one owner to another almost on a routine basis. Pepsi had merged with Frito-Lay a decade earlier, and was by the 1980s a diversified, but balanced food company. Coca-Cola had also diversified into juices, wine, and coffee, more or less successfully. Philip Morris, perhaps seeing these examples, acquired Seven-Up in 1978 for a big premium, and then managed to rack up huge losses in 1980, 1981, and 1982. By 1985, Philip Morris was looking for a way out. Pepsi volunteered, but encountered FTC resistance for the U.S. operations. In a period of five years, Dr Pepper would be sold (all and in part) a couple of times, Canada Dry twice, Sunkist once, Shasta once, and A&W Brands, Inc. once. Some of these deals were trades among food companies, but several, Dr Pepper as one example, were leveraged buyouts by investment firms. At the same time, many formerly independent bottlers were being absorbed and merged. The net effect was even stronger domination of the market by the two soft-drink giants.

WHO GOES FIRST? THE ADOPTION DECISIONS

The diet brands had been fighting it out, with everyone sensing that this market segment was going to become even more important in the future. The second major move by Coca-Cola was made in 1982 when it attached its name to a brand other than its original formula. Diet Coke was rolled-out using saccharin as a sweetener, but it quickly claimed a secure position in the market. Saccharin was not a happy solution because of the taste and warning labels. Although Abbott Labs, one of the largest producers of cyclamate, kept plugging away trying to change the FDA's position, that day seemed distant.

Approval of aspartame in Canada in 1981 had provided both Pepsi and Coke with opportunities to test aspartame in that market, and the numbers coming out of that market kept staring them in the face. Not only did Diet Pepsi taste much better with aspartame, but something very interesting was also happening. The bans had reduced diet soft-drink consumption to only 2 percent of the total market by 1979, down from 8 to 10 percent. Diet Pepsi was relaunched using aspartame and did very well, Diet Coke even better. By spring of 1983, the diet segment had grown to 21.3 percent of the market.[8] Aspartame could make the market grow! The economics were crummy, though. At $85 to $90 per pound, a rough estimate of what it was going to cost in the United States, aspartame was going to wreck margins. Still, if the stuff could grow the total size of the market, then the cost could be more than offset.

Learning to Play Hardball

Coca-Cola and Pepsi had initially supported NutraSweet's FDA petition by helping to find answers related to aspartame's use in liquids. Neither firm had made the final decision to adopt aspartame yet. The National Soft Drink Association, the industry's lobbying vehicle, had so far taken a mildly positive position. It was waiting for signals from its dominant members, Coca-Cola and Pepsi.

Shapiro began making the rounds, first in Purchase, New York, Pepsi's headquarters; then in Atlanta, Coca-Cola's home. The smaller companies like Royal Crown were ready to sign up, and Squirt and Crush brands were ready to go 100 percent aspartame. Procter and Gamble, which had had a contract dated in 1974, simply dusted it off for both Hires and Crush. Shapiro knew, of course, that either Coca-Cola or Pepsi had to jump, but he also knew that NutraSweet's capacity was not adequate to take on both of the giants at once. He was telling executives in both companies precisely that. Consistently and firmly.

He was frustrating some of these executives, from all accounts. For example, Enrico recounts in his book the NutraSweet position initially offered. Shapiro's terms were simple: adopt first and be assured of supply, and let NutraSweet determine the most appropriate blend for the product, even if that means 100 percent aspartame versus a saccharin/aspartame mix. Aspartame would be priced on a sliding scale—the more used, the better the price. The reaction was predictable. Letting an unknown, tiny new company dictate formulation to Pepsi was not only undesirable, but crazy in Enrico's eyes!

NutraSweet was coming across as a little brash. The prevailing attitude in the industry was "Who do they think they are? Didn't they know who they were dealing with?" The same questions were being asked by food company executives in other markets, as well. William Baar, vice president of Borden's dairy division, would later remark that NutraSweet's terms were ". . . not what we are used to dealing with in buying ingredients."[9]

What the soft drink executives didn't understand was that NutraSweet wasn't just any old ingredient. The experiences with diet drinks in Canada, and with products like Kool-Aid in the United States, were proving their point, the NutraSweet marketing staff felt. NutraSweet could help increase the size of a market, more than off-setting any price differential. This was the message being put across.

Neither Coca-Cola nor Pepsi wanted to jump, but both knew that the one that did would be able to gain a competitive edge of weeks or months in their ongoing war. Other food companies were signing-up, and the larger the customer list got, the shorter the supply potentially became. Despite the resentment the marketing and brand management people may have felt, the technical staffs in both firms were saying the same things to these executives. Aspartame tasted better, and was coming through the regulatory process with greater supporting data than any other sweetener could possibly hope. It was a standoff, and who would go first was a big, big decision.

What came next is one of the still confusing incidents involving NutraSweet's entry in the cola wars. The National Soft Drink Association (NSDA), at Don Keough's suggestion, and with Dick Wurtman, the MIT researcher's assistance, drafted a letter to the FDA after the wet use approval's announcement in July 1983 saying, in affect, to give final approval if, and only if, the FDA was totally behind aspartame. The letter's official intent was to express the industry's concern, but would potentially delay the final approval to be granted on August 1.

The benevolent view of this letter is that it was a sincere statement of concern by the NSDA. There was a lot of money at stake and some major brand names to protect. Depending upon your point of view, however, the letter was also either another chip for the companies to use in negotiating terms with NutraSweet, or it was, as Roger Enrico mused, a wonderful device for slowing down the adoption decision in Pepsi. The FDA quickly rejected the premises of the NSDA letter and gave final approval on August 1. Coca-Cola promptly announced in the trade press that it had made the decision to adopt aspartame and had a contract in hand, leaving Pepsi with the grim prospect that it couldn't get enough aspartame to meet Coke's preemptive strike. So much for cooperation in the cola wars. Pepsi quickly followed Coca-Cola's lead.

The new diet blends using aspartame were very successfully introduced. NutraSweet's sales had been dramatically improving as other food companies made adoptions, but the impact of the Coke and Pepsi adoptions were profound. Sales moved from less than $100 million in 1982 to almost $400 million in 1983, and over $600 million in 1984. However, the soft drink companies had seen that they could have the best of both worlds, lower cost and better taste, by blending saccharin and aspartame, down as low as 15 percent aspartame.

NutraSweet's branded ingredient strategy was taking hold by then, and the company was requiring customers to use the NutraSweet name and logo on labels. Only customer-blended product using aspartame exclusively could use the brand name and logo. Having to advertise someone else's product on their containers was hard for companies like Coca-Cola and PepsiCo to accept. Nonetheless, they were getting the benefit of aspartame's safety, as well as NutraSweet's advertising subsidies, by going along with the labeling provision. NutraSweet was happy to let them use blends because there simply wasn't enough product yet to go around. University Park and Augusta were still gearing up, but would soon come on-line.

A happy day, indeed, when production did finally crank-up to full capacity. The NutraSweet Company was now able to supply some of the smaller customers who had patiently stood by the company in the interim. The new message delivered to a less than receptive soft-drink company audience was simple: to use the NutraSweet brand name and logo they had to now go to 100 percent aspartame. The attorney general of New York had even independently taken action in 1984 by telling soft-drink companies selling in that state to either remove saccharin completely from their retail diet brands, or stop using the NutraSweet name. Deceptive advertising, the New York attorney general called it.

Sergio Zyman, one of Coca-Cola's negotiators, was reportedly flabbergasted when Shapiro broke the news. Pepsi wasn't any happier, since the 100 percent formula would require four or five times more aspartame, and the extra costs would have to be shared with bottlers. The compromise was that fountain diet drinks could still be a saccharin/aspartame blend, but no use of the NutraSweet brand name and logo would be allowed. Nonetheless, the move to 100 percent aspartame for the retail market segment was a chance for Pepsi to recoup some of the momentum lost by its slow initial adoption. Pepsi moved first, beating Coca-Cola to the market with the 100 percent aspartame product by only a few days. The impact on NutraSweet was almost immediate. In 1985, 8,228 pounds of aspartame would be sold to the soft-drink companies, versus 3,360 pounds in 1984.[10]

NutraSweet had entered the cola wars. In doing so, however, the company created a lasting legacy of resentment which it is still working to overcome. The question occasionally asked around Deerfield headquarters is whether the situation could have been managed any other way. Everyone was learning as they went, and the players in the soft-drink industry were as tough and seasoned as could be. Perhaps the moral to the story is that it is hard to be loved by everyone all the time. The bold negotiating posture had paid off, and the company could now move ahead with enough cash to create its own future . . . whatever that would be.

CHAPTER 6

LEARNING THE RUNNING GAME

We need to get our machine guns pointing
down the hill, instead of up the hill.
—*Bob Shapiro*

The soft drink adoptions marked a major transition point for
NutraSweet. Cash began pouring into the company, yet the
sudden success was also sharpening the pressures felt from
rapid growth. The young organization was being pushed even
closer to its limits. NutraSweet had to manage its rapid growth,
a challenge every young venture had to master if it was to last
in the market. Complete failure was never a prospect for
NutraSweet; the patent and demand for the product would
assure that. Instead, the fear was that the company would never
live up to its potential, and the patent would be licensed away or
the company would be sold if the organization didn't manage its
growth well.

Our culture idolizes rapid growth. In reality, too much
growth, too fast can kill a young venture as easily as having its
products or services rejected in the market. Often a crash later
in a lifecycle is harder because more careers and money are at
risk. Management systems, people, and organization structures
have to change quickly enough to accommodate new customer
demands, the entry of hundreds of new employees, and the more
general problems associated with increased scale. Apple Computer, DEC, and a host of other successful firms have had to deal
with the same issues. It was NutraSweet's turn.

A culture based on intense personal experiences among a
small group of people in the early years also gets diluted by
rapid growth. NutraSweet's culture had been dedicated to play-

ing David against food industry and regulatory Goliaths. Some of these giants had now become valued customers, if not partners in several markets. The net result was an acute identity crisis until a viable new culture began emerging. Shapiro's quote opening this chapter illustrates the change in thinking that was required. The "hill" had been taken by the troops, and now it was time to secure and defend their gains.

Not only did NutraSweet have to become proficient at serving aspartame customers, but the clock ticking away on the patent meant that Act Two, the next great generation of new products, also had to be designed. Too many single product companies were unable to innovate well enough to preserve themselves beyond the lifecycles of their initial, and only, market successes.

Classic marketing strategy would argue for doing as many product extensions and applications as possible for aspartame to prolong its life and broaden the scope of the firm. However, the days of high protected margins were clearly numbered. The foreign markets promised to be a major source of future growth, but competitors were already active in these. NutraSweet's margins were being compressed in those markets to keep competitors from gaining a foothold. Aspartame would quickly head for commodity status if the branded ingredient strategy failed, and the name of the game had to be remaining the world's low-cost producer.[1] Reining in the cherished start-up mentality would be necessary, yet that prospect didn't sound like fun to anyone then in NutraSweet.

Meanwhile, Searle's leadership was coming to the conclusion that Searle was at its own major transition point. This management team had stabilized Searle, and Don Rumsfeld now wanted to take a much more strategic view of the firm. What he found wasn't encouraging for a firm Searle's size. Searle was a medium-sized company at a time when size meant more and more. The pharmaceutical industry was fundamentally changing, and competing against the giants of the industry was becoming horrendously expensive. Searle may have been spending $2 million a week on R&D, but other major drug companies were spending $6 million per week on R&D. The days of the lone researcher making a new product breakthrough were over; large multidisciplinary teams fighting it out for a decade in the regulatory process were now the norm.

Three options were considered over the next two to three year period: maintain the present situation, merge with or acquire another drug firm to build scale, or sell the firm. NutraSweet couldn't be expected to carry the rest of Searle, so the first option wasn't perceived viable. Merging or acquiring another drug firm was considered, but the foundation controlling the Searle family stock wanted to diversify its holdings and actually sell some stock. Selling the firm became the most serious option.

One perception that can be dispelled is that Don Rumsfeld and John Robson were brought into Searle only to groom it for sale. This scenario is not accurate. True, Don and John both saw themselves returning to government service or teaching at some point. But they waited eight and a half years before thinking about leaving. In an age where the average CEO tenure was five years or less, the Searle management team had paid its dues. The Searle family's interests had always been an important concern during this time. They had even engaged Dan Searle and the board in a series of pro/con role-playing sessions to test the sale idea. Searle as an acquisition candidate was taken off the market by Rumsfeld after Monsanto passed on it the first time.

Monsanto came back to take a second look late in 1984, although Dick Mahoney, Monsanto's CEO, was reportedly very leary about this thing called NutraSweet. Indeed, the presence of NutraSweet had reportedly made Searle unattractive the first time around. Monsanto wanted access to the pharmaceutical industry, not the sweetener industry; it wanted to get out of commodity chemicals and into more innovative products and industries. NutraSweet was generating free cash flow, but the stream of earnings was also potentially going to dry up in the mid-1990s.

Nonetheless, the $2.8 billion sale was finalized in August 1985. NutraSweet thus found itself with a new, much larger parent with uncertain intentions. Ajinomoto, not surprisingly, quickly volunteered to alleviate Mahoney's concerns by offering to buy NutraSweet. Ajinomoto's offer was fortunately rejected because NutraSweet has proven to be the jewel in the acquisition. It would be late 1989 before the Searle pharmaceutical business would turn a profit and residual law suits were settled concerning Searle's copper IUDs.

From 1985 on, life for NutraSweet became even more complicated, not less so. It had to secure its position in its core business to prepare for 1992, create Act Two, and negotiate a place within Monsanto. Shapiro and his management team had to create an organization with a long-term future. This chapter tells what happened as they went about doing that.

"SMALL PEOPLE" BECOME IMPORTANT

Depending upon who you talk to, NutraSweet's history is divided into three more or less distinct stages. The first stage ended with the FDA approvals, and appeared to be dominated by the "lawyers and finance types." The second stage is just ending, and has been dominated by legal, marketing and sales, and manufacturing groups functioning at a much more strategic level. Big choices were being made in every functional area; the legal group was working on the patent extension, marketing was dealing with the soft drink adoptions, and manufacturing was making very basic technology choices. Looking back on this second stage, the prevailing attitude seems to be, "Hey, I guess we kind of pushed them a little too hard, so we'd better give them whatever they want."

The rhetoric in the emerging third stage sounds more self-confident and determined in the characteristic, older NutraSweet style. Uniquely, this third stage centers around the line managers and staff deeper in the trenches in marketing and sales, manufacturing, R&D, and units like government affairs who make less dramatic choices each day, but must now fine tune the organization. The attitude starting to be expressed in this stage is, "Many of them (our customers) will really never love us, so let's be so darn good at what we do they can't do without us."

Where Rumsfeld, Robson, and Shapiro—all the "big guys"— may have been most deeply involved in engineering events in the first stage, the burden has been shared in the next two stages with those further down in the company. As George Logan, now managing director for Middle East and Africa business, once commented in a conversation, "This company was built upon 90-yard passes in the Superbowl—really big plays. We're now having to learn 'first-down football' and the running game." A lot of things have to happen all at once now, and progress was going to be incremental, not transformational. It is going to take the concerted efforts of a lot of "small people," both old and new, in all parts of the company. NutraSweet is feeling the need to become more like a normal organization.

REDESIGNING THE COMPANY

While that need is real, Bob Shapiro was determined that NutraSweet would never become truly normal. He felt comfortable using conventional management models when appropriate, but overlaid those with radically different design principles whenever possible. Recognizing the need to lay a foundation which could accommodate growth, Shapiro restructured NutraSweet in October 1988. It changed from its historical functional structure, which was appropriate for a single-product firm, into a classic three division structure, which was more appropriate for a multiple-product firm. The goal was to also flatten the organization by pushing decisions further down. The second division created in addition to the NutraSweet division centered around Simplesse, still early in its development and very different in the technology used to produce it. The third division was Business Ventures, a new product development group. Several corporate level groups would support these three divisions. The new structure is illustrated in Figure 6–1.

The important point about the new design was that it reflected the commitment to staying in the food industry. It also reflected a much more complex strategy. The transition from a single business to a multibusiness company can be traumatic. A whole new way of thinking is required. New management processes and systems are also needed to manage the exponential increases in complexity. The design trick is to define a core unifying theme and basis for competitive advantage which cuts

FIGURE 6–1

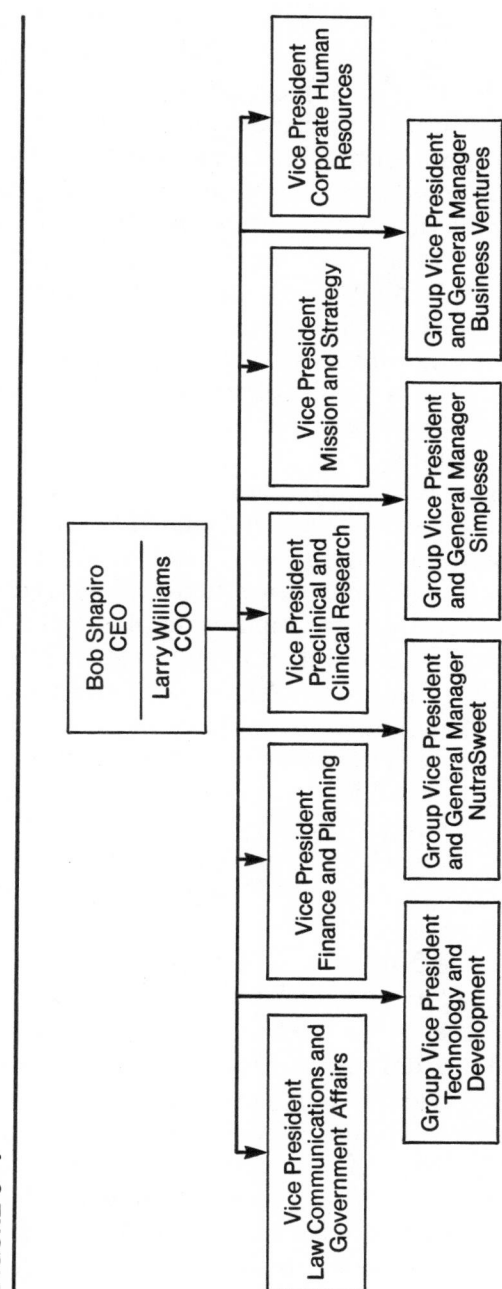

across divisions. For NutraSweet, a set of basic design principles appears to guide this process, as Chapter 8 discusses.

The design principles overlaid on the conventional design don't show up in a two-dimensional diagram. That is the problem with organization charts, of course; they've always been poor representations of multidimensional realities. These over-laid design principles have intentionally created tremendous tension and uncertainty for people used to working in "normal" organizations. In Bob's eyes, the goal is to perform high quality tasks routinely without the people and the company ever becoming rigid—creating order within controlled chaos, in other words.[2] Again, Chapter 8 discusses several of these principles in detail. The objective here is to illustrate what was done, more than how it was done.

The agenda was pretty well set. Five areas of highly interdependent activity could be identified. Within the aspartame core business, NutraSweet had to (1) strive to stay a low-cost producer, (2) develop a much stronger customer service orientation, (3) continue finding new applications for aspartame, and (4) become the dominant international competitor. Nothing ambitious here, right? The fifth activity area centered around R&D and the critical need to find the next products for Act Two.

All of these activities were to occur within the context of Searle's acquisition by Monsanto. Much to its credit, the dominant role consistently played by Monsanto has been that of a supporter and facilitator. True, it has been able to recapture much of its intangible goodwill investment in Searle through NutraSweet's success. On the other hand, where other firms may have drained NutraSweet's cash flow, Monsanto has given Shapiro whatever resources he has needed to prepare his company for the future. That was a smart thing for Mahoney to do, according to John Robson. If Monsanto had created aspartame, John once half-seriously suggested, the result would have been pricing aspartame like a generic chemical and selling it at one-tenth the price that Bob Shapiro was able to get with the branded ingredient strategy. It made sense for Dick Mahoney to give Bob room to move with ideas like that one.

Mahoney also moved to give NutraSweet even further autonomy by separating it entirely from Searle, while salting a few key executives into the NutraSweet structure to build depth in key areas like R&D and marketing. Larry Williams, an experienced branded products executive from Philip Morris, was, for example, made president and chief operations officer (COO) of NutraSweet in November 1986. The prevailing attitude is that Shapiro has free-rein to experiment and run NutraSweet as long as performance holds. If it doesn't, as Bob has said, "I expect to have lots of offers of help."

BECOMING THE LOW-COST PRODUCER

One of the most painful episodes in NutraSweet's present history has centered around the cultural and organizational change induced by the implementation of a low-cost producer strategy for aspartame after 1992. When it comes to being the low-cost producer, NutraSweet is, of course, already in this position. With its innovations in the manufacturing process, NutraSweet produces from all indications lower-cost, higher-quality product than even Ajinomoto. The coupling technology for aspartame's two components was further improved in 1987, along with improvements in both L-phe and L-aspartic production. The company now closely guards its proprietary process secrets and even clouds perceptions about true costs and margins. It is thus best positioned to succeed after the patent falls, having ridden the experience curve further than any of its rivals. It also has the money to spend and expertise to do it. Monsanto approved in 1989 the doubling of manufacturing capacity at a cost of more than $100 million.

The fundamental issue was actually whether to even become a low-cost producer or not. Remember that it wasn't clear until 1986–87 that the company had a long-term future at all. Successes with new aspartame applications, the penetration of several international markets, and progress with Simplesse began convincing everyone that staying for the long haul could make sense.

The company found that it could innovate internally and compete effectively; the company wasn't just an artifact of a lab accident protected by a patent; it was here to stay. Costs were reduced by over 50 percent in five years, while prices had fallen domestically only 35 percent in the same time period. As a result, 1988 margins were the highest in history, with the improvements flowing directly to R&D and operating income.

But competitors were also gearing up. By announcing its investments in manufacturing and R&D, NutraSweet was posing the question to potential competitors: "Who wants to ride prices down the furthest?" Was this a bluff? Personally, I don't think so. The company's aggressive marketing and pricing practices in Europe are testimony that the question was meant as a legitimate challenge. If NutraSweet was able to stake out the low-cost position first, then it could slow its rivals' entries.

A second motivation for becoming the low-cost producer had to do with Shapiro's definition of aspartame as a replacement for sugar. If the cost of aspartame could ever get lower than that of sugar, then customers would consider using aspartame instead of sugar. This was a huge, huge market with volumes potentially able to more than offset the loss of margin on smaller volumes. An intriguing idea, to say the least.

Monsanto has been immensely helpful in securing NutraSweet's low-cost position. Monsanto had been one of the original producers of saccharin and had left that business, but it knew something about sweeteners. It certainly has the process technology experience from running large facilities, coupled with a long history of working with younger bio-technology firms through strategic alliances and partnering arrangements. A few NutraSweet engineers gave a sigh of relief when Monsanto acquired Searle. It seems that one or two process designs had been "borrowed" from Monsanto years before, and the joining of the two firms eliminated any doubts about ownership. Now it was all in the family. At present, Monsanto helps when asked, and the competence of its engineers makes it easy for NutraSweet managers to ask.

Much of the challenge in becoming a low-cost producer isn't technological or financial, but cultural. As I noted in an earlier chapter, the tension between the goals of a start-up operation and low-cost production is intense. The values expressed by low-cost production become juxtaposed against those of the other, more familiar culture. For example, where an innovative culture encourages individual risk taking and experimentation, a low-cost production ethic in a continuous-process bio-technology facility makes risk taking and experimentation difficult. As Don Minarich, vice president of Manufacturing, commented in response to my question about whether there can be entrepreneurial behavior in manufacturing, "Yes, but in supporting areas like human resources, not in the process technology." Innovation on the process side couldn't be initiated without a broad-based team approach. The slower than expected start-up of the hybrid process at Augusta had demonstrated that point. There was little room left for one person or one group to independently initiate changes in the increasingly complex processes.

On the other hand, the bureaucracy that many feared the much larger Monsanto would bring to NutraSweet was being turned to advantage in several ways. For example, Monsanto once requested that the number of different job and pay grades be reduced to make the two organizations' human resource systems more comparable. Rather than view this as a hostile act by the new parent, NutraSweet used it as an opportunity to expand the job scope and content of the impacted positions. More discretion and autonomy were provided, not less.

The low-cost production emphasis would, nonetheless, also show up in budget requests that would be forwarded to, and then scaled back, by "corporate" while production goals would be increased at the same time. It's an old story, of course. Most people understand the need to wring slack out of an organization that just went through a period of "blank-check" expansion. But this kind of situation was precisely what many of the young manufacturing engineers and managers in the plants had left previous companies to avoid.

NutraSweet would have to find a way to make the transition in cultures. There would be some inevitable loss—some people would go on to other companies to do start-ups simply because that's what they liked best. Hopefully this number would be small. Once the limits and capacities of the facilities were gauged, more realistic budgets and forecasts also could be generated and accepted. Multidisciplinary teams would also be used more to tackle process changes. And the focus for innovation would need to shift to making incremental refinements and improvements to in-place systems. A Total Quality Program is being instituted, for example. Ironically, this program is being implemented in manufacturing settings which are already producing at pharmaceutical grade standards that don't exist elsewhere in the food industry. The Total Quality Program does serve another important purpose; many of its basic tenets about empowering workers and stressing quality are parts of the NutraSweet Mission Statement. The program operationally fits NutraSweet, unlike many more traditional manufacturing companies that have had to work hard at changing an entrenched culture to implement the program.

Yet with all of these adjustments, there is still the need to preserve the best aspects of that original start-up mentality. Becoming a low-cost producer means adding capacity; the doubling of capacity underway at Augusta and a planned facility for a foreign market will require that very same culture which served so well at the beginning in Harbor Beach, University Park, and Augusta. Finding the balance between the demands posed by the two cultures is an ongoing challenge. The conscious decision is to favor one set of values more than the other at a point in time, depending upon the needs of the organization at that time. The great challenge within the company is to figure out how to move swiftly and effectively from one to another without unavoidable disruption. It is uncomfortable and confusing for many employees if they don't understand the choices and reasons for change. The tension between old and new does raise, however, the question about the relationship between strategy and culture, a topic discussed in detail in Chapter 8.

CREATING CUSTOMER SERVICE

Perhaps no area needed greater attention than customer service. There has been considerable progress in this area, but lost ground is hard to recover. Brand new customers wouldn't understand the concern about customer service. The older ones do. As Bob Shapiro was quoted in a November 1989 *New York Times* article, "I'm sure that there were times when we were rude or inconsiderate and that we said things we shouldn't have said, or failed to say things we should have said. I know we've changed . . . to some degree."[3] The pressure to build the company quickly had exacted a toll.

The petition process used by the FDA is unique because it asks approval for specific applications of a new ingredient. NutraSweet had gone to the FDA for dry use approval with General Foods and for wet use approval with the soft-drink companies. You would think that the intimate hand-holding required by the process would provide the basis for a warm, lasting relationship between the companies involved. True, General Foods and the other early friends are held dearly within NutraSweet, but the histories of the approvals have shown how the best of friends can strain their relations.

When a company joins in a petition, it does so for its own self interest—getting a jump on its competition. The day NutraSweet starts offering product and process expertise to those competitors, the petitioner's temporary competitive advantage is lost. The fellow-petitioner may also end up waiting in line with its competitors for scarce product. Alas, this situation occurred because no one guessed how much aspartame would actually be demanded. Everyone in NutraSweet was startled by the demand that was created. The dramatic increase in demand caused by the soft-drink adoptions compounded the problem.

The patented use, branded ingredient strategy, 100 percent aspartame requirement, and direct advertising to consumers also antagonized some customers. The perceived hard-nosed, "take it or leave it" sales approach some food company executives felt that they had encountered were not forgotten. Others appreciated NutraSweet's strategies. Smaller customers benefited from the logo and advertising support since these helped them compete against larger competitors.

Despite whatever negative reactions may have resulted, NutraSweet had a compelling need to get as many adoptions as possible. A broad product base offered more protection when the patent expired. This meant that continuing company assistance was absolutely essential for testing new customer applications and providing technical support for them. Aspartame also had two inherent problems; it was not stable over long periods in liquids, and it broke down into its constituent parts when heated. Working with customers to prolong product shelf life and to overcome the cooking use limitation was critical.

The easy part of improving customer service is to get the parts of the company interfacing with customers to improve the quality of those interactions. In marketing, for example, it means quoting availability and price accurately and quickly. It also means understanding what customers are trying to achieve with their products and helping them achieve their goals. Customers are routinely asked for promotional ideas which NutraSweet subsidizes. In manufacturing, support means getting high quality product to the customer in the most efficient, convenient form. If a customer wants "just in time" delivery in 50 kilo bags, so be it.

Developing a dedicated, sincere commitment to customer service is possible and is being done by a great many companies, including NutraSweet. NutraSweet has built a group of about 25 customer service and sales staff to manage the company/customer interface. This group and the customer account managers do more than simply make sure that an order is filled, however. Building confidence about product availability is one of their functions because some customers had stockpiled product to prevent shortages, thus tying up their assets. The regulated, technical aspects of aspartame also mean that this staff has to provide technical assistance, regulatory counsel, and potentially extensive market research for customers. You can't leave these tasks totally up to customers to perform if you're going to make a sale of a product like aspartame.

The Technology & Development Group

The real trick is to interface internal R&D with customers to help them develop new applications and work through technical issues. Here is an area in which NutraSweet excels, in my opinion. The Technology & Development Group, as it is called, is now one of the largest groups within NutraSweet with more than 200 people, 190 of them professionals with 65 percent of these holding the Ph.D. degree. It is presided over by Mike

Losee, a soft-spoken corporate scientist with 18 years of development experience in Monsanto.

In 1987 alone, this group received over 4 percent of total sales as its budget, when standard food industry R&D expenditures were 1 percent or less. Its budget was allocated across three prime objectives: lowering costs, finding new applications for aspartame, and developing new products. Some of the group's output is totally mundane improvements in process technologies at a plant level, while some of it is truly *science-push*—ideas for which someone has to figure out a commercial use. Simplesse was one of those ideas. Still, those three objectives reflect a pragmatic assessment of NutraSweet's situation. According to Losee, the company's only true barrier is time, and the group's objectives reflect the allocation of R&D resources to the present, near future, and distant future. His strategy, as a result, is to get a hundred different things going, and then winnowing away those that don't best fit those objectives. The trick is to kill a bad idea early enough so that resources can be quickly reallocated.

Barry Homler loves working on the applications side of this group. Homler was one of the early pioneers in NutraSweet, having initially been involved in the 1970s explaining aspartame in "dog-and-pony" shows around the country with Annette Ripper, a dietician. Barry was a scientist first, but has had an intense interest in seeing how aspartame is used by customers. He had worked on the first dry use applications and petition. Barry is now head of a group called Applications Technology, which initially had as its sole mission figuring out how many different uses there are for NutraSweet's products. Lately it has begun working more with the Business Ventures Group.

Some of Losee's research groups play with 3-D color models of hypothetical molecules created by supercomputer-driven software. Parts of Homler's offices, on the other hand, smelled like bean burritos and baking pies when I visited him. NutraSweet runs food labs in the United States, Canada, and Europe to test new applications. One afternoon while waiting for Barry, I listened to a receptionist phoning potential taste-tester consumers to schedule them in to try something else the lab had concocted. The vivid contrast between the 3-D modelling and baking burritos was a reminder about what hi-tech food companies were all about. Some Betty Crocker types may have been in Barry's kitchens, but they were being backed up by Ph.D. bio-engineers and dieticians on the other side of the building.

I asked Barry what he was doing about the shelf stability problem that required soft-drink companies to periodically rotate store stock. What he provided was a colorful vignette of a soft-drink truck rolling through the desert in 130 degree temperatures toward Las Vegas. While 95 percent of the product is consumed within the recommended 12 weeks' shelf life, a Southern California independent bottler was dumping product after 7 to 8 weeks, thinking that the extreme heat speeded-up the process. This, in effect, was jumping costs to the distributor.

NutraSweet technical support staff suggested a study to see what was really going on. Temperature recordings were made from time of production until time of sale using recorders that were placed on the trucks, in the cartons, and in bottles for three aspartame and sugar-sweetened products. The results showed that the shelf life wasn't 12 weeks, but 6 months. Several other unrelated changes in the distribution process were also recommended to further cut the bottler's logistics costs.

Another vignette illustrates the way NutraSweet works with food companies in the regulatory process. The costs to a small company of filing a new use application can be a serious obstacle in an adoption decision, so Homler's group helps here, as well. A fruit juice producer resisted adopting aspartame in its fruit juice boxes due to an FDA requirement. The FDA said that aspartame would have to be added to juice heated at 275 degrees for 45 seconds. This was a serious hurdle since it could ruin the juice. Instead, the producer would have to put aspartame into sterile boxes, a time-consuming and expensive step. NutraSweet helped perfect a heating and aspartame addition process that let the FDA requirement be relaxed. The entire juice industry has subsequently adopted the process. NutraSweet got the sale, and the juice producers got a cheaper blending process.

The emerging pattern is for NutraSweet to work with a customer in perfecting technical issues, performing sensory evaluation studies (taste tests), and writing and filing a petition. In a few cases, like baked products, NutraSweet has done much of the up-front work, and has then found customers to adopt the results. A company with a pharmaceutical-industry orientation and extensive regulatory experience, coupled with a collaborative approach to working with customers, is unique in the food industry.

So, while the early days of getting adoptions may have been perceived as a little too assertive for some customers, there is now a highly-developed, "close to the customer" approach within the company. The trick is to be useful to customers so that the old ones forget any unpleasant early memories, and the new ones come to expect a level of service which no competitor can easily duplicate.

COMPETING INTERNATIONALLY

The typical pattern for most firms is to develop an international presence by first succeeding at home, then making sales abroad, and then gradually deepening their presence in a foreign market through direct investments. Once they actually begin producing in other countries in wholly- or partially-owned facilities, they've become multinational enterprises.

NutraSweet doesn't fit this pattern for several reasons. NutraSweet had to think like an international company from the start. The company quickly learned that consumer consumption patterns, regulatory law, and specific product applications varied country by country, and that these differences had to be mastered if the company was ever going to be more than a U.S. phenomenon. The earliest final approvals were also in other countries, notably Japan, Canada, and in Europe. The first sales were outside the United States, as a consequence. Approval was gained in September 1983 in England, for example, and by the end of 1984 there were more than 100 products in that market containing NutraSweet. The patent also expired in those countries around 1987, thus forcing NutraSweet to deal with competition outside the United States first.

Given the early relationship with Ajinomoto, the company also adopted an early perspective on the global manufacturing and distribution process. Ajinomoto, however, was not a major actor in Europe; NutraSweet drove the entry into those markets. With the August 1989 announcement that it was building an aspartame plant in Brazil, and its continuing consideration of a possible plant in Europe, NutraSweet is moving toward multinational enterprise status.

It isn't just a historical accident that NutraSweet has had to think and act internationally so early in its life. Its largest customers in the United States are multinationals themselves. Coca-Cola, for example, derives the majority of its soft-drink revenues from outside the United States, and when it wants to move more strongly into Brazil, for example, NutraSweet is compelled to also think about Brazil. And as these giants know, the fastest growth is in these international markets. NutraSweet was selling aspartame for products in the Soviet Union and Brazil for the first time in 1988. The growth rate in Australia was 21 percent in 1988, contrasted to the relatively mature markets in the United States.

Brazil hates imports, however, particularly of sweeteners that would replace sugar, a major export crop. But Brazilians are increasingly following the global trend of becoming more diet and health conscious. They would drink a diet-brand soft drink, but the Brazilian government would like Coca-Cola to use an artificial sweetener developed from the stevia plant which grows locally. The problem is that the stevia-derived sweetener tastes terrible.[4] The solution, of course, is to put an aspartame facility in the country which could use local inputs, bring new technology into the country, and generate export sales.

The same types of situations arise in Europe, where U.S. food companies often need to modify blends and flavors. NutraSweet has a food lab in Europe to partially support their U.S. customers' efforts to modify their products for local tastes. They provide the same services for European food companies, as well. So, a company is international because its customers are international.

Also keep in mind that Shapiro's definition of NutraSweet's aspartame business is as a replacement for sugar. That definition takes you into some unusual markets. Take China, for example. As I mentioned in an earlier chapter, there aren't many fat Chinese; the conventional use of aspartame for reducing calories isn't even a concern. Instead, China imports sugar that must be paid for with scarce foreign exchange. Locally produced aspartame is potentially cheaper than imported sugar when all of the costs, including interest and opportunity costs for the funds, are factored in. This market is years away from becoming a reality, but it does illustrate the international implications of the sugar-replacement strategy.

While these reasons are logical in explaining NutraSweet's international activity, the most obvious and compelling motivation is the fact that its most threatening potential competitors are international, not domestic. Table 6–1 summarizes several of the major competitors and their sweetener products.

There are strong potential domestic competitors with alternative sweeteners, such as Pfizer's alitame. Sucralose is another. These products are in various stages of the regulatory process, each having unique features that make them better or worse than aspartame.[5]

The list of potential international competitors is large: Green Cross, a Korean chemical company; a couple of Italian chemical companies; Holland Sweetener, a joint venture between Dutch State Mines and Toyo Soda of Japan; and Hoechst Celanese, the giant German chemical company that competes in the table-top market in the United States via a joint venture with Cumberland Packing. The Korean, Dutch, and Italian companies produce aspartame. However, the Koreans and some of the Italian companies will likely never emerge as serious competitors due to their lack of sophisticated process technology and quality control.

No one likes to talk about it much, but one potential competitor that could be added to the list is Ajinomoto, NutraSweet's own long-term partner. Ajinomoto has manufacturing facilities in the United States—a plant in North Carolina and one in the midwest. These could likely be converted to produce aspartame. That is a sad prospect to ponder at the NutraSweet Company. The preferred belief, which is well-grounded in Ajinomoto statements, is that Ajinomoto and NutraSweet do so well together internationally that there is simply much more to be gained by collaborating rather than competing.

Also add to the list of potential competitors large customers who would like to break away from aspartame, or at least improve their negotiating positions with NutraSweet after their

TABLE 6–1
Short and Sweet

The Major Artificial Sweeteners Summarized

Sweetener	Trade Name	Price per Pound	Sweetness (x sugar)	Attributes	Legal Status
Saccharin	Sweet 'N Low	$4	300	Aftertaste	Available in United States because of Congressional moratorium on proposed FDA ban warning label required
Aspartame	NutraSweet	$80	180–200	Unstable at high temperatures; cannot be used in cooking	Available in United States
Cyclamate	n/a	$8	30	Low sweetening power	Banned in United States in 1970; currently under consideration for reapproval
Acesulfame K	Sunnette	unknown	200	Aftertaste, but potentially strong product.	Available in United States
Alitame	n/a	unknown	2000	Stable at high temperatures, highly soluble in water.	Pending FDA approval
Sucralose	n/a	unknown	600	Good water solubility and stability.	Pending FDA approval

contracts expire. The most significant example is The Coca-Cola Company. Coca-Cola announced in December 1988 that it had discovered a new family of left-handed sweeteners that were 1,900 times sweeter than sugar.[6] Coca-Cola has a patent, but has not yet chosen to put the discovery through the FDA.

Another earlier form of left-handed sweeteners, as a side note, was the result of an accidental discovery in 1976. A sample was being sent on the Viking lander to Mars as a food source for any alien life, and a scientist happened to taste the substance. A small bio-technology company, Biospherics, is still struggling to get this form of sweetener through the regulatory process.

Discovery is one thing, of course, and toughing it out in the regulatory process is something else. For Coca-Cola, betting cherished brand names on an artificial sweetener that no other competitor is committed to is risky. But Coca-Cola's point is clear to NutraSweet, and it appears serious about future experimentation, as well.

If you ask NutraSweet executives, they would argue that some of their competitors have acted downright unethically. The Koreans jumped the patent expiration date in Canada. The Italians produced aspartame for Searle in the early days, and still do some production for NutraSweet in Europe, but they also produce and directly sell aspartame in countries that don't recognize Searle's U.S. patent.

The most bitter battle, however, is with Holland Sweetener. NutraSweet is presently being sued by Holland Sweetener for dumping in Europe, and is even questioning NutraSweet's U.S. patent validity. The Canadian government in late 1989 also stepped into a complaint brought by Tosoh, Holland Sweetener's Canadian subsidiary. The Canadian government is inquiring whether NutraSweet's 95 percent share of its $30 million aspartame market is an abuse of a dominant market position. Whether meant as irritants or entirely seriously, the law suits point out the intensity of this conflict.

The irony of this particular competition is that it is Holland Sweetener, not NutraSweet, that is crying foul. It claims that NutraSweet is practicing a "scorched earth" policy of selling product below cost and of discrediting Holland Sweetener's viability. Keep in mind that NutraSweet's international partner is Ajinomoto, a company also known for competing aggressively. The two partners market so effectively in Europe that the list of customer adoptions continues to grow despite competition.

A close look reveals that their success is due to more than price cutting. Customer service through food labs like Barry Homler's, reliable distribution, and a high quality, available supply are big factors in getting the more conservative European food companies to try aspartame. There have been new adoptions in Mexico, Korea, the Philippines, England, and even Holland. France was opened as a market for the first time in 1988. Nonetheless, the price of aspartame has fallen to $27 a pound in Europe due to price competition. NutraSweet claims that it is still making money at that price.

One view of this conflict is that Holland Sweetener is simply trying to appear wounded enough so that the European Commission will restrain NutraSweet and Ajinomoto, thus helping lock-up Europe for a "national champion" just as European integration takes shape. NutraSweet has a basic problem with Holland Sweetener's legal strategy. It doesn't need a competitor building large-scale economies in a protected European market so that excess capacity can then be used to export to the U.S. market. NutraSweet's marketing strategy has even been called by some industry observers "Not one kilo" in reference to the company's determination to keep competitors from gaining a significant foothold in the U.S. market. That means keeping the pressure on in Europe to keep competitors off balance. Note how the company's international and domestic U.S. actions reinforce each other.

The same pattern of intense competition exists in Canada where Tosoh has successfully taken a customer, Schweppes, away from NutraSweet. Ken Dooley, Tosoh's vice president for sales, is quoted in the November 19, 1989 *New York Times* article as saying, "Their strategy is simple. They want to eliminate competition."[7]

Judging from NutraSweet's history, that statement is not entirely accurate. It is more accurate to say that NutraSweet ethically does what it needs to do to compete successfully in a market; if competitors fail, that's not NutraSweet's fault, but the market's choice. The difficulty some critics have with aggressive marketing strategies is that it is hard to separate the earned benefits of dominant market position from unfair competitive practices. Firms around the world strive to achieve dominant positions in their markets, and when they should be penalized for achieving that advantage is far from clear.

What's really so important here is how NutraSweet has learned to compete. NutraSweet learned a great deal about how to compete from its international experiences. It is bringing that experience home just before the U.S. patent expires and faces competition here. This is a flip from the conventional way U.S. firms compete; they traditionally take lessons and skills developed in the United States to foreign markets, not the other way around. At the close of 1989, 22 percent of NutraSweet's sales came from outside the United States, and its stakes in international markets will grow, not shrink. The challenge will be to become a global producer, not just an exporter, to take advantage of the sugar replacement potential of international markets, and to ride a growing global health-consciousness wave.

CREATING ACT 2

A tremendous amount of cash flow is being directed at new product development. I'm not sure what the figures actually are for new product development alone. When you figure the size of Losee's R&D group, and number of staff and professionals within Linda Gohlke's legal and government affairs group, Frank Kotsonis' clinical research group, and the two new product divisions devoted to creating Act 2, the numbers are "large."

NutraSweet's basic premise is that being a low-cost, value-added producer of aspartame is essential, but so is creating entirely new products. With the announced introduction of Simplesse in January 1988, NutraSweet was trying to make some of that investment pay off. The substitute or "fake fat" market is estimated to be as large as $15 billion, with NutraSweet potentially being able to generate, according to some analysts, up to $500 million in sales by the mid-1990s.[8] Monsanto's stock even jumped a couple of points after the Simplesse announcement.

Note that this figure doesn't match the magnitude of the sweetener markets. While the company may be bullish on the post-patent market for aspartame, the search for even more products has to continue. Larry Williams' announcement in October 1988 that the company was reorganizing into three divisions was meant to set the stage for this ongoing search. Simplesse would become a division headed by Dave Morley and eventually be organized much like NutraSweet's aspartame business. The focus of these two divisions was on overcoming technical issues, creating efficient commercial-scale production processes, and, very important, working on product applications. The more far-out, still fuzzy business ideas would be the domain of Tom Burnet in the third division called Business Ventures.

Inside Simplesse

The FDA finally approved Simplesse in late February 1990. Simplesse isn't just another product for NutraSweet—it is living proof that NutraSweet is not just a one-product company flash. It broadens the scope of the company by entrenching it further within the food industry beyond simply sweeteners. Simplesse is completely consistent with the company's mission of bringing "better food choices to consumers through the application of advanced technology" (see Appendix B for the NutraSweet mission statement). Its psychic value at least equals its economic value.

Simplesse has been called "fake fat" because it can be substituted for fat in foods and yet provide the taste and texture of fat. It is synergistic with aspartame—low calorie/low fat cheesecake is a reality and a symbol of that synergy. Simplesse has several additional similarities and differences with aspartame which have profound implications for NutraSweet, the company.

The more spartan, somewhat chaotic offices dedicated to Simplesse are located in Skokie, a few miles away from the beautifully subdued Deerfield headquarters. You immediately notice the youthful climate of Dave Morley's shop, even more so than that of the generally youth-oriented headquarters. I reminded myself, upon entering the Simplesse offices, to begin a search for anyone over 50-years-old that I could find in the company. Dave is himself a young Purdue M.B.A. with a biology degree. After spending several years in Searle, he came over to NutraSweet to bring Simplesse beyond the concept stage.

Dave pointed out several important features of Simplesse and their implications for The NutraSweet Company. It turns out that the process to produce Simplesse came to NutraSweet via Norm Singer, a John Labatt Ltd. researcher, who joined NutraSweet to work on aspartame. In 1979 Singer had observed a substance forming from emulsified egg white in part of a Labatt cheese plant's process. The stuff tasted something like cream cheese and intrigued him enough to experiment with it. He found that it had very few calories—about 4 calories per gram of protein versus 9 calories per gram for fat. He remembered it later when he moved to NutraSweet in 1983 and managed to get the technology bought from Labatt. Labatt retains the Canadian rights to Simplesse.

What was so nice about the substance, later to be named Simplesse and given a soft blue and white logo, was that its constituent parts were GRAS—generally regarded as safe—and therefore, it was assumed, not subject to the same regulatory scrutiny as aspartame. The much shorter regulatory process was both an asset and a liability. It made it easier to get into business, but it shortened the learning curve tremendously. The company knew everything there was to know about aspartame by the time it was finally approved, but they would be in the market with Simplesse with many questions still unanswered. On the other hand, there was an organization with scale and resources behind Simplesse, where they had to create one for aspartame. Aspartame also provided many lessons for Simplesse about marketing and production; reinventing the wheel wasn't necessary.

Because the components were commonly available, it was the process technology to create the creamy texture that was patentable. Basically, what the process did was take skim milk and egg white proteins and blend and reduce them to an almost molecular level. At that size, the resulting substance passed through the mouth with the same textural qualities as fat. In effect, Simplesse fools the tongue. Compared to aspartame, however, the relatively simple process technology made the product more vulnerable to competition. Writing the patent application therefore became a legal exercise in creating defensible space and barriers in as complex a maze as possible, something the legal group in NutraSweet took great joy in executing. There are many ways to be creative.

There are also relatively fewer customers and competitors for aspartame than for Simplesse. The range of uses for Simplesse are an order of magnitude greater than aspartame. While getting the soft-drink adoptions were aspartame's key to success, figuring out the best entry point for Simplesse was tougher. Which products and markets were the most profitable, offered the best defense, and could be leveraged into additional products and markets were less obvious.

The potential customers for Simplesse were most of the food companies which, it so happened, were also working like crazy to introduce their own versions.[9] Kraft had been working on its own version, but decided in August 1989 to become NutraSweet's first big customer by adopting Simplesse. Frito-Lay, the huge PepsiCo division, CPC International, and Unilever, among others, are also experimenting.

Procter & Gamble had Olestra, which was a man-made chemical substance unlike the GRAS ingredients in Simplesse. The difference is important because it meant that P&G had to follow the tougher and longer FDA approval process. Olestra had a greater range of uses than Simplesse, which made it a potentially tough competitor if approved. Procter & Gamble also had 80 people assigned to its development and marketing.

Procter & Gamble had not managed the regulatory process well for Olestra, having apparently failed to learn from NutraSweet's experience with aspartame. The patent has even expired on the product—no last-minute, "one-legged Hopi" patent extensions for Procter & Gamble. Much of the delay possibly could have been avoided. It seems that P&G first went after the pharmaceutical applications for Olestra, and thus spent precious years of the patent life looking at applications in that industry, not the food industry. This is surprising since P&G is, above all, a consumer products and food company. Observers are saying that it will be at least 1995 before Olestra will show up in the market.

Morley and the rest of NutraSweet respect the competition facing Simplesse, yet here, too, I found the same "high confidence" which characterized the early marketing of aspartame. That attitude generally serves the company well, but it has resulted in two important decisions that proved in one case to be a tremendous *faux pas*. Because Shapiro and the other top NutraSweet executives assumed that Simplesse's ingredients were GRAS, then the FDA did not need to review the product. The company had greatly improved the flavor of Simplesse with its R&D. NutraSweet was altering the physical, not chemical, properties of the ingredients.

They had forgotten, nonetheless, the political environment that the FDA had to function within, and that they were NutraSweet, still one of the most controversial companies in the food industry. Frank Young, the FDA Commissioner was reportedly outraged that NutraSweet, a company he had stuck his neck out to defend in the past, would try to bypass the regulatory process. As a result, Simplesse was tied up in a regulatory review for over two years. Was the FDA being punitive, as some industry observers suggested?[10] Not necessarily, but you can bet that NutraSweet will be more careful about making assumptions regarding the FDA's right to screen products.

The second major decision which has become controversial is due to NutraSweet's growing belief that it can compete very effectively against slower moving food companies. The pharmaceutical heritage of the firm has given it a depth in the sciences, along with a rigorous approach toward product development and customer support that the food companies couldn't match. Its successes in Europe and Canada with aspartame were also reassuring. A technologically sophisticated, flexible, and aggressive marketer has a place in the food industry. This, at any rate, is the premise the company is increasingly operating with as it looks at end-use food industry markets.

This premise logically takes NutraSweet to the idea of introducing food products of its own, either with its own label or through a private label company. Equal, the tabletop sweetener, had been taken directly to the consumer, so there was a precedent. *Advertising Age* had also reported in February 1988 that a secret marketing plan was being floated to repeat that success with other products. Why get the profit from only selling the ingredient when you can have the whole thing? Add to the marketing plan rumor the fact that Simplesse was developed without help from another food company, unlike the close hand-holding that routinely occurs with aspartame.[11]

Either the company seriously believes its assumptions, or we are once again seeing competitive posturing on the usual grand food-industry scale. The prospect for a food company was to either adopt Simplesse or face a competing product. The true position is a mixture of both possibilities. Morley and Shapiro honestly believe that Simplesse can be sold both as an ingredient to some customers, and also taken directly to market through captive products which compete head-on with those of other food companies.

The rumor was true, of course. Simplesse was rolled-out in February to very positive media and market response in Simple Pleasures, NutraSweet's own frozen dessert product line produced and distributed by Dreyer's. A four-ounce serving of Simple Pleasures contains 120 calories and 1 gram of fat versus 250 calories and 15 grams of fat for regular ice cream. In characteristic NutraSweet fashion, the traditional food industry rules have been examined and rejected. Still, making food is different than making ingredients. There are plans to license Simplesse to food companies, using the same branded ingredient strategy as with aspartame. Kraft is already prepared to move into the market, for example, with several products carrying the Simplesse logo.

Franchises for All?

Business Ventures under Tom Burnet has its own ideas working, but these are meant to be exploratory and a longer term challenge to the company. Business Ventures scans the world for new product and business opportunities. The ideas which get airing in Business Ventures are meant to test basic assumptions and ways of thinking which could then move the company off in a very different direction several years later. The ideas are meant to be co-produced with other customers as much as possible. They come from customers, or are given to customers to think about.

Desserve—The Sampler Cafe is a 40-seat shopping mall restaurant concept now with two locations near Deerfield. NutraSweet is in the restaurant business, tentatively but successfully from initial appearances. Desserve is an attempt to pull good-health food items together into a limited menu. Several items use NutraSweet, but many do not. The menu is cholesterol-free, low fat, low calorie, and meant to be enticing—chicken salad, chocolate mousse, pumpkin chiffon pie, etc.—with calorie counts listed by each item. Yes, they cater.

Industry analysts give the idea mixed reviews.[12] The company doesn't know much about the restaurant business, they argue, and retailing is, indeed, a long way from being an ingredient producer. The analysts miss the whole point. Of course it is an alien industry for NutraSweet, but had that ever stopped the company before? How else is the company going to learn about consumers, products, and other ways of competing? The whole thing is one great big learning experiment. Who knows, they may make money, too. Shapiro and Burnet playfully, but also half-seriously, suggest that Desserve may be one way for NutraSweet employees to get a piece of the action. They see no reason why employees can't be given Desserve franchises if the concept makes financial sense.

SUMMARY

The Business Ventures group has other more secret projects at work, as well. The point is that NutraSweet has tried to frame the demands for internal innovation into separate action time frames, with Burnet's group taking the longest view. Business Ventures is concerned with Act 3 and beyond. Morley's Simplesse group is deep into its own market entry, and has tremendous needs for testing additional product applications—much more applied innovation. Back in Nick Rosa's NutraSweet division, the name of the game is to perfect production technologies to beat the costs down ever further, while also providing value-added customer support. Losee's R&D group services all three divisions, and his unit's internal structure reflects the orientations of those three divisions and their strategies.

This is life in NutraSweet now. The present company is a much more sophisticated organism than the loose group of 10 or so scientists and marketing types struggling within Searle to make the first sale of aspartame in 1974. What the company has become is a product of the conditions and of the playing field on which it competes. The terrain of this playing field needs closer examination before turning back to the design principles Nutra-Sweet has adopted as it continues to evolve.

CHAPTER 7

THE NEW PLAYING FIELD FOR INNOVATION

> Science seldom proceeds in the straightforward logical manner imagined by outsiders. Instead its steps forward (and sometimes backwards) are often very human events in which personalities and cultural traditions play major roles.[1]
>
> —*Dr. James D. Watson*

Let's step back for a moment and put the NutraSweet story into the larger context of three fundamental social forces driving corporate innovation and social change. It is important to understand how extremely powerful, pervasive, and therefore meaningful, these three forces are for innovating corporations like NutraSweet. For example, it was the cultural trend toward health consciousness and nutrition which helped create the "fear of fat" that largely made the company possible in the first place. But aspartame didn't just ride this cultural wave, it amplified it. Aspartame's use as a sweetener is essentially meaningless if taken from the larger cultural context of the time.

The interactions and dynamic tension among the three forces described in this chapter have, in turn, set in motion dramatic shifts in the governing norms and ways corporations go about the process of product and process innovation. Opportunities are created and killed through these shifts. The companies that understand them, and use them, are at a distinct competitive advantage over companies that do not. These paradigm shifts are also briefly described in this chapter. Several important authors have eloquently explored several of these shifts in a number of books; there is little need to duplicate their efforts, only to summarize some of their basic premises and note their importance for innovation within NutraSweet.

The net result of this brief exploration is hopefully a better appreciation of why the design principles used by NutraSweet are so different and important compared to those used previously and by other companies. It is too easy to look at a single-company case study that has been taken out of its larger context. The next chapter looks specifically at the design principles used by NutraSweet using a conceptual framework which can apply to other companies, as well.

THE THREE DRIVING FORCES OF INNOVATION

It is practically impossible to grow up in the latter half of this century without a curiosity about technology and social change. Much of my past decade has been spent trying to piece together an understanding of the technological and social context in which organizations grow and adapt. Probably the most important contributors to this contextual appreciation have been the academics and writers spanning the intersection of social change, technology, and government policy. Foremost among these for me is Daniel Bell, the Harvard sociologist, who authored *The Coming of Post-Industrial Society* and *The Cultural Contradictions of Capitalism,* among others.[2] Jacques Ellul, the French sociologist who authored *The Technological Society,* is also an important contributor, along with the less well-known but prolific Lewis Mumford, author of such books as *Technics and Human Development: The Myth of The Machine.*[3] There have been a host of others, as well, including Alvin Toffler of *Future Shock* fame.[4]

All of these authors were writing at a time in which there was deep, general concern about the pace and direction of technological change, the impact of this change on the society and culture of America, if not the world, and the role of government in managing that change and those impacts. These concerns weren't new. Henry Adams in 1918 was even writing about "social physics" in an attempt to understand the impact of science on early American society.[5]

These authors' attempts at explaining what was happening to "Spaceship Earth," as Buckminster Fuller called it, are also fun to read just to see how close some of them have come in their projections. Some have come close, indeed. Take Daniel Bell's concept of "postindustrial society," for example. As the services sector of the U.S. economy surpasses the industrial sector in employment and contribution to GNP, you are forced to conclude that Bell was accurate. While specific events are hard to forecast, the more general trends and tendencies many of these authors tried to describe have largely proven true.

What is clear is that there is a dynamic, often unstable and unbalanced, tension among three interwoven components of our present predicament: technology, culture, and government. If you are trying to understand the dynamics of any present situation, in other words, it is useful to try to understand how these three elements play a role through their interactions. Figure 7–1 illustrates their relationships to each other.

Technology

By technology, I mean the knowledge and skill base, not just tools and techniques, prevailing at a point in time within society. Technology has a life of its own. Scientists, engineers, and technicians add to the knowledge and skill base and create new tools/techniques continuously. The rate of addition is not linear but exponential. New contributions are driven by the inherent human passion for scientific inquiry and the desire to answer unanswered questions.

FIGURE 7–1
The Three Forces Driving Innovation

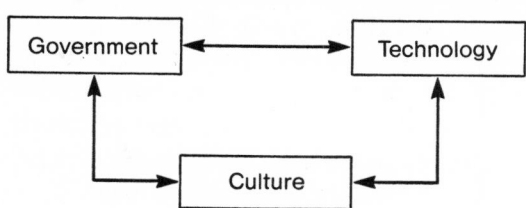

Technological innovations also arise in response to cultural demands and opportunities. These contributions are perhaps motivated by capitalistic values and imperatives such as the need for improved profits, greater efficiencies, and higher quality. The "new and improved" syndrome is indemic in a capitalistic culture that generates wealth like ours has since World War II. Jeremy Rifkin, one of the most outspoken critics of bio-technology, makes an excellent point when he talks about the impact of computers on human life:

> We're now organizing time below the threshold of participation. You cannot perceive a nanosecond, or experience it. What happens when a civilization organizes itself on a timeframe below the realm of actual experience? You can't participate in it.[6]

Technology is therefore value loaded. It is partly the result of cultural demands and needs, but it also creates them. Technology creates and shapes possibilities and expectations. It is what Edward Wenk, Jr., author of *Tradeoffs: Imperatives of Choice in a High-Tech World,* calls a *social amplifier.*[7] Again, NutraSweet is an obvious example. As another example, no other forms of technology have played as strong an amplifying role as communications and information technologies have played. More information made more accessible is both a benefit and bane. We have been able to create organizations of global scale and tremendous flexibility, and inform people about a greater array of choices than ever before. On the other hand, we can bury ourselves in information which, in reality, has little practical value. Richard Saul Wurman describes a new condition he calls *information anxiety* which is "the black hole between data and knowledge and what happens when information doesn't tell us what we want or need to know."[8]

What we are confronted with, Wenk contends, is the question of whether we can manage technology, not whether we can accomplish something through technology. In an insatiable culture, technological innovation potentially has no limits. The question of control rests with government and is in the realm of science policy. Take the question of new food additives or drugs, for instance. "How safe is safe?" was a question posed in a previous chapter, and the answer was that "science is a moving target"; *safe* is, for better or worse, situational and relative to the prevailing culture.

Culture

There is a lot of interest in corporate culture over the past four or five years, because a positive, supportive culture is seen as essential to successful strategy implementation. Culture in the three-component model illustrated in Figure 7–1 refers to the larger societal concept of culture (i.e., American Culture). Culture is a tough concept to define, but the definition provided by Daniel Bell in *The Cultural Contradictions of Capitalism* is useful. He describes culture as,

> a continual process of sustaining an identity through the coherence gained by a consistent aesthetic point of view, a moral conception of self, and a style of life which exhibits those conceptions in the objects that adorn one's home and oneself and in the taste which expresses those points of view. Culture is thus the realm of sensibility, of emotion and moral temper, and of intelligence, which seeks to order these feelings.[9]

A complex definition, for sure, but useful because it recognizes the dynamic quality of culture and how it is manifested within a society. Bell thinks of culture as a *process* of making sense of one's world through tangible objects, as well as emotional and moral positions adopted to deal with situations that arise. Culture is, in other words, a way of expressing the values and beliefs adopted by people for dealing with their world.

An important aspect of culture which was often not considered by earlier writers is the role of demographics—the sheer number, type, and location of people within the society. The infusion of new European, Latin, and Asian minorities into the traditional American society over the past 20 years, as well as the next 20 years, is having a profound impact on our traditional conception of American culture. We still don't understand the full implications of this demographic trend.

Another important demographic trend is the aging of the population, including the so-called baby bust following the baby boom. This generational shift has already had many spin-off trends, such as our intensely heightened health consciousness. Shifting demographics profoundly impact culture in terms of how we feel about, and what we want for, ourselves and others. Companies like NutraSweet try to identify and ride those trends with products and services, naturally, and they have gotten pretty good at doing so. A smaller, more diverse work force also puts pressure on corporations to create and adopt new, more efficient manufacturing technologies and ways of designing work, as well.

Government

Government, regardless of political ideology, is deeply engaged in decision making that impacts the demand and supply of products and services we want. Government sets the rules and conditions under which goods and services are exchanged to satisfy wants. Government is also concerned with the satisfaction of other important values and needs, such as our sense of justice and equality.

The important question about government is its capacity and ability for managing the complexity imposed by technology and the competing demands posed by citizens responding to diverse cultural imperatives. To what extent should and can government intervene in managing the interactions between culture and technology? The concern expressed by many, of course, is that government does not have the capacity, resource wise as well as intellectually, to manage this complexity and competition.

The Interaction of Technology, Culture and Government

This is, up to now, an academic exercise in describing the sources and regulators of social change. The bottom line, to be more practical, is that the corporation must actively manage and shape to greatest advantage the outcomes of the interactions among the three forces described above.

The interactions among these forces are powerful enough to sweep any corporation along with the currents that are generated. As an illustration, I like to use the example of the youth revolution of the late 1960s and early 1970s. The Vietnam War was a product of government policy, and would never have been as aggressively challenged if it were not for dramatic, relatively sudden shifts in cultural values. What was driving those value shifts? A new social awareness and elevated sense of social responsibility? Yes, of course, but what brought about the new awareness? Technology, I will argue, not some inherently humanistic or spiritual state achieved simultaneously throughout American society. Television brought the war to our living rooms, electronics made "revolutionary" rock music accessible to masses of people, and chemistry, through widely available, powerful drugs, altered perceptions of the prevailing reality. The 1960s were a coincidence of interacting forces, not a consciously designed and managed social process.

Government has never been the same after this time period. Our culture was also altered for decades, whether for the better or not. Concerns about our environment and health have survived the subsequent two decades and have become major trends every corporation has been impacted by. These macro-level interactions thus pose critical contingencies for the corporation striving to grow and compete in its markets.

The interaction between government and culture is so close and deep as to almost be inseparable. Conversely, government shapes culture by regulating what we see on television, what we have available to purchase, and at what prices (due to taxation policies). I'm not talking about command economies like the one now breaking down in the Soviet Union; I'm talking about so-called market-driven economies like our own.

Similarly, government is a regulator and promoter of technology. Government patents innovations, sponsors research and development, regulates the entry of products and services into markets, and so forth. Technology also shapes government. The availability of a particular technology to apply to a social problem will determine policy toward that problem. As a ready example, the feasibility and cost of "Star Wars" technologies clearly impacted the U.S. bargaining posture with the Soviets through the late 1980s.

Bringing this entire discussion back to corporate innovation, the interaction of the three above driving forces has had obvious implications for NutraSweet. The technological innovation called aspartame would have had little impact or utility if the prevailing culture had not been supportive. The health consciousness that began in the late 1960s became so intense that it even kept saccharin on the market despite damaging research. People wanted an artificial sweetener because staying thin and avoiding sugar was perceived healthy. Government's role as regulator and facilitator of culture and technology is also apparent. The FDA was the gatekeeper which regulated the introduction of aspartame into the culture. The forces are real. The challenge is to work with them to your advantage.

SEVEN PARADIGM SHIFTS

Without question, the types of interactions I'm concerned about have very visible manifestations. These manifestations are visible as long-term, fundamental shifts in the conditions and assumptions governing how innovation occurs. There are at least seven of these paradigm shifts, as I call them, and they provide leverage for managing the dynamic environments companies confront. Figure 7–2 lists the seven shifts. Each of these shifts is described next, along with their implications for a company like NutraSweet.

From Machine Age to Organic Thinking

Russell Ackoff, a Wharton School professor, was among the first writers to describe the fundamental scientific shift from viewing the universe as a well-ordered machine to that of a highly organic system of dynamic, integrally related parts.[10] It was a shift from reductionism to systems thinking, which paralleled the emergence of the natural sciences, particularly biology. Basic to this shift is the recognition that problems need to be

FIGURE 7–2
Seven Paradigm Shifts

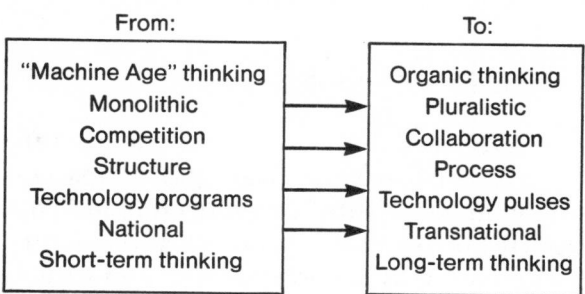

From:	To:
"Machine Age" thinking	Organic thinking
Monolithic	Pluralistic
Competition	Collaboration
Structure	Process
Technology programs	Technology pulses
National	Transnational
Short-term thinking	Long-term thinking

understood in terms of their larger context, not reduced to constituent parts that in themselves give no perspective on the entire problem. You gain understanding of a problem by placing it in its larger context.

The shift to more organic, systems thinking has several practical implications. First, organic thinking de-emphasizes *analytic* skills—which stress finding a single right answer—to *appreciative* skills—which emphasize asking the right question. In a world of infinite information and maximum uncertainty, asking the right question may be more important in directing energies and effort.

Organic thinking places a new product into a larger cultural context of social, political, and economic conditions and forces that determine how it will be used and valued. Aspartame, in this perspective, had social, political, and economic dimensions that transcended its immediate use. It was not simply an artificial sweetener, but a product which fit an emerging lifestyle, posed tremendous technological and scientific uncertainties for the FDA and food companies, and was the economic foundation for a much larger NutraSweet.

Innovators therefore have a responsibility to appreciate as much as possible the larger context in which their new products and services are introduced. Performing an internal "impact analysis" is also a wonderful exercise because it can uncover additional applications and positive spin-off effects. This responsibility is particularly important for the emerging Hi-Tech Food Companies of the future like NutraSweet, as Chapter 9 discusses.

From Monolithic to Pluralistic Models

Inherent in the "machine age" model is the view of the organization as a bounded fortress with well-defined boundaries between what is inside and what constitutes its environment. The closed-system conceptualization of the organization is fortunately breaking down. The notion of boundaries was a machine age, bureaucratic fantasy from the beginning; the organization's boundary from its environment is a sieve, at best.

The organization is an open system in deep and constant interaction with its environment. For example, a firm's employees certainly don't live entirely in the firm; more of their time is actually spent outside than inside the firm. Viewing employees from such a one-dimensional perspective has been dangerous and expensive for companies in many respects, such as excessive job turnover and drug abuse.

Organizations have stakeholders which claim legitimate interests in the way an organization conducts its activities. Corporations have numerous stakeholders such as customers, creditors, suppliers, government regulators, and employees. Indeed, as Jeff Pfeffer, a Stanford professor noted, there is the very real danger of an organization becoming "externally controlled" by the proliferation of its stakeholders to the point that internal management loses effective decision-making control.[11] What is going on is power sharing.

There is, conversely, the danger that a corporation not recognize the impact that its stakeholders can have. The American auto industry, for example, has been criticized for being blind to its customers' needs. Ford has made a bold, assertive bid to reconnect with its customers, and has fared much better in terms of its performance over the past four years. The other auto makers are still trying.

Overall, the shift toward more pluralistic forms of organizational governance means that power sharing is inevitable. Centralized, unilateral control doesn't work as well as in the past. AT&T's break-up and the deregulation of transportation means that market forces will govern interactions among organizations and groups in the society.

What corporations need to accept, then, is that a different set of skills will be required to effectively compete in a pluralistic economy. Diverse, coexisting interests dictate development of effective negotiation, conflict management, and communication skills to create shared interests. Confrontation simply doesn't carry the corporation as far as it would perhaps like to think. For example, American manufacturers are now actively working with suppliers to coordinate inventory levels through programs such as a "just in time" system. Coordination can produce better long-term results than constantly coercing suppliers to lower their prices to a point where they are weakened financially and can no longer innovate, and thus provide improved supplies.

The NutraSweet story provides several vivid examples of the costs of not collaborating and benefits of collaboration. Playing hard ball with the soft-drink companies may have been necessary at the time, but certainly has some costs associated with the practice; customer loyalty is a virtue as the patent expiration approaches. On the other hand, the close, highly effective collaboration between the food companies and NutraSweet (described in the last chapter) illustrates the value of sharing effort and resources.

From Competition to Collaboration

The costs of a "go it alone" mentality, with its view of the corporation as a fortress, are simply too high for most corporations to continue paying. We have learned from the Japanese that coordinated, long-term, targeted strategies executed across a set of companies and governmental players can be effective in improving the competitiveness of the individual players involved. Collaboration is becoming a core part of corporate strategy, particularly as industries take on global scale. Michael Porter and Mark Fuller, a Harvard professor and a consultant, respectively, note, for example, that "While coalitions are not new in international competition, their character seems to be shifting. Coalitions are becoming more strategic, through linking major competitors together to compete worldwide."[12]

An excellent example of the importance of collaboration for innovation is provided by Olivetti, the giant Italian electronics company. Olivetti has had to recognize that it was at a severe competitive disadvantage compared to American giants like IBM. It accepted the idea that it could not work at the leading edge of a technology through internal R&D alone. In 1989 it articulated a radically new strategy regarding innovation. It would become a platform for new technologies and products brought to it by others, thus emphasizing its own marketing and distribution strengths. Olivetti has direct controlling and minority stakes in 200 smaller technology-based companies throughout Europe and the United States. It will also work with Japanese manufacturers in introducing their Olivetti-branded products into its markets. These are truly the days of joint ventures and strategic alliances.

While much of the collaboration is occurring among otherwise competing groups, there is increasingly close collaboration all along the value-added chain, from suppliers all the way through to customers.[13] If a particular activity within the corporation does not directly contribute to the value of a product or service delivered to a customer, the increasingly prevalent view is to out source that activity—that is, let someone else do it that can provide it less expensively or with better quality.

The net effect of rationalizing the value-added chain is the proliferation of relationships that have to be managed, and better-focused, higher value products and services. Again, this is equivalent to a shift toward more market forms of organization, away from the monolithic, totally vertically integrated corporation. There is an excellent question, of course, whether we know how to effectively manage such complex networks of interdependencies.

The corollary to market-based collaboration within the firm is, of course, the idea that divisions and business groups need to collaborate, not compete in executing strategy. While it is often motivating and efficient to have three manufacturing plants compete on the basis of their performance, the competition becomes tremendously dysfunctional when the three plants are integral parts of a larger corporate strategy which requires harmonization of their activities. Efficiency, which may contribute to the loss of effectiveness in penetrating new markets with new products, may not make good strategic sense.

Similarly, competition and conflict between technical and marketing groups can kill the commercialization of an innovation. Corporations deal with the threat of internal competition by introducing a variety of linking mechanisms between the groups involved, offering group-based and multifunctional team rewards, creating cross-training opportunities, and sharing data bases to minimize the barriers created by internal subcultures.

From Structure to Process

The pace of technological and industry change makes the erection of structures of any kind comparable to creating the Maginot Line in anticipation of World War II. The flexible, adaptive, fast company is the one that wins in today's markets. Maneuverability and the ability to have maximum impact at a chosen point in the market can count more than scale. As George Gilder points out in his controversial book, *Microcosm,* a study of the semiconductor industry, new products have come much more from smaller, entrepreneurial companies, than from the largest of the high technology companies.[14]

Gilder is criticized for his support of entrepreneurism in an American industry which must compete against Japanese industrial giants like NEC and Sony. Smaller companies, the critics argue, don't have the market clout to penetrate markets deeply enough to sustain share once the Japanese load on. On the other hand, the larger firms can not create an internal environment which is flexible and creative enough to allow broad-based, continuous innovation to occur. These larger firms inevitably get hardening of their internal innovation arteries.

This is a complex issue, yet the lingering perception is that large scale leads to hierarchy which, in turn, unintentionally slows innovation. The rapid pace of industrial change diminishes the importance of large scale in penetrating and holding markets with new products. This is, of course, not to say that a large scale of operation and command over plentiful resources aren't important for a company, only that *sufficient* scale is necessary; *excessive* scale serves no useful purpose other than to raise overhead costs and slow reaction time.

Information and communication technologies have radically facilitated decision making and speed of response for managers. As another consequence, the movement toward collaborative networks of companies serving a single large customer or an entire market has become possible. What we now see is unitary, well-defined organizational structures giving way to *flows* of information and services across their boundaries.

Putting large-scale project and program structures in place to manage the innovation process can be useful in a great many instances, say creating a new commercial spacecraft. But managing the innovation process in a dynamic, highly competitive marketplace requires accepting what Robert Waterman, Jr., author of *The Renewal Factor: How the Best Get and Keep the Competitive Edge,* calls *stability in motion*—continuous, incremental change.[15] The design objective is to provide sufficient structure to create a basic order, but to prevent structure from getting in the way of processes which respond more quickly to market needs.

Process is increasingly a substitute for structure. For managers, this means learning how to become excellent process facilitators, including negotiators, communicators, and conflict managers, with a high tolerance for uncertainty and change. It also means that people, along with their skills, abilities, and commitment, are more important to the company than rules and policies. What a wonderful prospect!

From Technology Programs to Pulses

The days of programmed and paced introductions of product innovations are over. As the amount of scientific knowledge grows and the technological base expands, the pace of innovation has also accelerated. With more intense competition among companies through their technologies, the flow of innovations into markets is becoming continuous, not discrete.

The past century can be characterized by episodic, spaced introductions of technological innovations. The automobile entered the economy and has only been partially replaced by the subsequent introduction of the airplane. There have been improvements in both of these innovations over time, but for autos, at least, these had been planned and consciously paced up until the last decade. Remember the new car unveiling ritual which was experienced with delight each year? Model years now vary from manufacturer to manufacturer, with new models coming into the market as soon as they can be designed and produced.

Newer technologies, such as bio-engineering and computers, are also being introduced and improved at paces which give the appearance of a cascading waterfall or the pulsating flow of blood through an artery. Competitive pressures dictate rapid introductions and follow-on product line extensions and modifications to ride experience curves as rapidly as possible to reap the benefits of prematurely shortened product lifecycles. New design technologies such as CAD/CAM and close user involvement in the design stage have also accelerated the pace of market entries. As John P. McTague, vice president for research at Northrop Corp., noted, "The more design and production become seamless, the better (off) we'll be."[16]

Continuous flows mean being internally organized in ways to work those ideas quickly and effectively through the groups involved. The Japanese have also understood the implications of this paradigm shift for some time. For example, they only take three years to bring a new model to market while U.S. auto makers take five years; the result is a fresher and greater number of models in a market.[17]

For corporations, pulsating technologies mean having a continuous flow of new ideas working internally. Active hunting for new ideas takes place outside the company, as well. Remember, NutraSweet barely got to the patent office ahead of Ajinomoto, which had heard about aspartame at a scientific conference. Staying informed about new developments, whether internally or externally, has taken on strategic importance. Many corporations have created the position of Chief Technical Officer to signal the importance of, and providing a focal point for, the innovation management process.

From National to Transnational

Markets and competition are now being defined along global, not domestic, dimensions. Several authors have explored this shift in great detail.[18] The objective here is to note that corporate innovation has also gone global. Indeed, Bob Shapiro noted in a conversation that "Molecules don't have nationalities." He was referring specifically to the challenge of competing in Europe against companies such as Holland Sweetener. Rather than viewing the competition in nationalistic terms—a U.S. company against a Dutch company—Shapiro was making the point that technological innovation and competition today knows no national boundaries. It is a serious error in thinking and strategy to create essentially artificial boundaries when none truly exist.

From a practical perspective, a global view of competition and innovation leads to specific decisions. For example, where to locate research facilities is an important aspect of corporate technology strategy, since the location decision determines how quickly product adaptations to local markets can occur and the foreign investment terms can be negotiated with host governments. The traditional co-location of corporate headquarters and R&D is antiquated.

Bob Shapiro's statement poses even more fundamental challenges, however. It suggests that some innovations, perhaps not all, but an important class of technologies like bio-technology, transcend national boundaries. We tend to look at global competition from the perspective of national rivalries—Japan versus America, for example—instead of appreciating how those technologies can be developed and deployed for global markets from just about any developed nation. The inherent advantage of locating in the United States is that its very large market helps to amortize R&D costs over long production runs, but greater European and Asian market integration is already underway. Steel technology was dependent upon accessibility to ore, coal, a well-developed transportation system, and population base. Bio-technology is not.

Technological innovations can now emerge anywhere, given sufficiently nurturing conditions. India and Saudi Arabia could, for example, become major players in bio-technology if they decided to give that area high enough national priority. Where the product innovations coming from that technology are introduced is a secondary issue. The important point is that there are many new technologies which simply don't have national allegiances.

In the never-ending search for comparative advantage, we have postured technological innovation as a "them versus us" contest among the largest industrialized countries. As the technological infrastructure of some rapidly industrializing countries (the RICs) and newly industrialized countries (the NICs) develops, the action-packed game of technological competition in the next century will welcome a potentially much expanded set of players.

From Short-Term to Long-Term Thinking

Last, but certainly not least as the saying goes, is a welcomed shift from economic rationality measured in three-month intervals to strategic performance measured over several years. The past decade in the United States has been devastating for corporations trying to execute major transformations. Ed Hennessey, CEO of Allied-Signal, was able to transform the old commodity chemical company he inherited into a major technological player active in several high-technology sectors over an 11-year period. Jack Welch is doing the same thing at General Electric. Motorola and The Black & Decker Corporation are also doing the same thing.

While wonderful to recount, you have to appreciate how unusual these stories unfortunately are. The number of executives who have had the time and opportunity to execute long-term strategic plans is much smaller than it should be. What's so disturbing is that this pattern is happening in some of our most vital new industries, not older ones. Genentech, for example, sold a 60 percent stake in 1990 to Hoffman LaRoche, a German firm, reportedly to allow it to get away from the constant glare of financial analysts and investors who wanted shorter-term results than its management was prepared to give.

The leapfrogging of the new technologies in industries such as bio-technology does lead to shorter product lifecycles and the rapid movement of companies into and out of markets. Part of the problem is also due to the amazing intolerance of the financial markets for long-term corporate strategy. A flood of readily available debt, and prospects of significant financial gain through leveraged buyouts, hostile raids, and breakups were enough to disrupt any CEO's long-term plans. No industry has been immune, and no corporation could afford not to have a defensive strategy mapped. A great many corporations were able to use mergers and acquisitions strategically, such as GE and Allied, but others either assumed more debt than they could handle or became victims to raiders. A classic tale of how short-sighted financial strategy destroyed a firm is told in Max Holland's 1989 book, *When The Machine Stopped: A Cautionary Tale From Industrial America,* a story about the destruction of a machine tool company named Burgmaster Corp.[19] Burgmaster was over-leveraged and unable to innovate in a market increasingly attacked by the Japanese.

The overall net result for the nation was diminished attention to R&D and internal innovation at a time when global competition was demanding more. R&D spending has fallen consistently since 1984, according to a *Business Week* sponsored study in August 1989.[20] After climbing 12.7 percent annually from 1976 through 1985, the inflation adjusted rate for 1989 is only 1 percent versus 1.3 percent in 1988 and 3.7 percent in 1987. Not good news.

More encouraging are four recent trends. First, the pace of hostile mergers and acquisitions is way off in 1989 and will remain so due to uneasiness about excessive leverage. This gives companies a little more relief from hostile takeovers. Second, the role models American corporations have chosen are corporations in countries which promote long-term strategy, specifically the Japanese. The moral is if foreign firms succeed for this reason, so can our companies. Third, corporate executives are also starting to listen to a few business academics and executives that are preaching long-term strategy. Michael Porter from Harvard, for example, emphasizes how financial measures of performance are not necessarily good measures of strategic health.[21] For Jack Welch, the performance of GE's businesses is measured in terms of their standings in their respective industries, not near-term ROI.

Finally, several technology-based corporations, NutraSweet among them, are realizing that manufacturing something gives control. Licensing technology away, or getting it from someone else, creates interdependencies and prevents the development of internal innovation capacity. There is nothing inherently unique about the technology licensor; there is certainly something unique about the company that manufactures and markets its own creations which were built from a deep technological competence built from that effort. For NutraSweet, it was uncomfortable having the young company's fate in the hands of another company, regardless how benevolent that company may have been at that moment. You simply don't put the future of your company into the hands of others. Period.

Whether these four trends are enough to lengthen executive time horizons and stiffen resolve is not clear. Corporations will need years to recover from the abuses and excesses of the past decade. They at least appreciate the need to change.

SUMMARY

The purpose of this chapter was to put NutraSweet's development into the larger context of several major forces and shifts which relate to corporate innovation. These forces and paradigm shifts worked on the young company in complex ways, but largely to its advantage. It is to Bob Shapiro's credit, as well as his top managers, that NutraSweet recognizes its impact and is able to design a company fit to meet the challenges it poses. The playing field for innovation when Searle first discovered aspartame's value is fundamentally different from the one Nutra-Sweet must play on now. The terrain of this field transformed before its managers' very eyes. While challenging, winning on this field is viewed by everyone in the company with relish. No one is bored.

But guiding a company through this terrain is still a formidable task. What helps make it possible are a number of design principles or governing assumptions that provide a way of thinking about the challenges facing the company. Most important, however, many of these principles focus on the people in the company. NutraSweet has not mastered all of these principles, nor are they final; new ones emerge to deal with a changing competitive reality. Chapter 8 turns to these design principles as lessons for other companies.

CHAPTER 8

DESIGN PRINCIPLES FOR AN INNOVATING COMPANY

> Entrepreneurial businesses treat entrepreneurship as a duty. They are disciplined about it . . . they work at it . . . they practice it.[1]
> —*Peter Drucker*

The types of paradigm shifts described in the last chapter were largely viewed as positives by NutraSweet's leadership. Shapiro and his top management team appear to understand the nature of these forces at work and use them to advantage. They welcome market "discontinuities" because they provide gaps and significant niches for their company which operates differently than industry norms.

It also soon became clear that Monsanto liked NutraSweet and the creative boldness with which the company attacked its markets. New aspartame applications were coming to market, there was exceptional progress in reducing cost, and Simplesse was being publicly launched. Dick Mahoney, Monsanto's CEO, was able to demonstrate to financial analysts just how well the Searle acquisition was working. So pleased, in fact, that he named Shapiro a group executive vice president in Monsanto in June 1990.

NutraSweet's leadership has managed a very open process of articulating, experimenting, and getting buy-in for the concepts wanted to guide the company into the future. Whether the employee is a unit supervisor in Augusta or Bob Shapiro in Deerfield, the company asks these people to think and to talk about their predicaments and choices. No one sits around all day talking grand theory; there is a strong action-bias within the company. A state of mind and an approach to problem solving is encouraged, which is difficult to characterize. Sir Geoffrey Vickers in his book, *Value Systems and Social Process,* would perhaps call it an *appreciative system*—an "ecological system" which interprets, orders, and develops a population of ideas that conflict, compete, and mutually support each other within the company.[2] Above all, it is an ability to place themselves, their work groups, and their company in a still larger context, whether in time, in relation to the industry, or in relation to all other organizations. There is an ongoing, interactive process at work within the company which explores the company's self-concept and choices. This is done through discussion and through very symbolic actions. The Desserve Cafes are symbolic of the company's willingness to experiment and learn about different ways of competing. Shapiro's "molecules don't have nationalities" comment is symbolic of the company's attitude about its domain for competition and place in the world.

There were moments, sitting in Bob Shapiro's office interviewing him, for example, when I felt that he could literally disappear, leaving his chair physically empty, but still have his concepts and ideas working away with a life of their own, surrounding us. And it wasn't just Bob; it was also Max, and Barry, and Mike, and Ralph, and any number of the other managers. You develop the sense after a while that these people *really* believe in the power of ideas to shape their organization's future. Which is, of course, the case.

There are a great many other young companies around the United States, and world, that emit the same aura of intellectual curiosity and enthusiasm. Their leaders have each learned some important lessons about how to design innovative, competitive organizations which are intensely achievement oriented. It's more than being competitive, and it's more than being innovative. It is the focused application of a competitive spirit and innovation together that is so striking. Kenichi Ohmae, head of McKinsey's Tokyo office and author of *The Mind of The Strategist,* offers this perspective:

> Insight is the key to this process. Because it is creative, partly intuitive, and often disruptive of the status quo, the resulting plans might not even hold water from the analyst's point of view. It is the creative element in these plans and the drive and will of the mind that conceived them that give these strategies their extraordinary competitive impact.[3]

The purpose of this chapter is to distill from the NutraSweet story some of the design principles used to foster that state of mind and give such impact. A few of these principles will sound like homilies because they have recently been heralded by other writers. This doesn't mean that they should be discounted; when a hundred different observers of companies say pretty much the same thing, it is more than "group think." Still other design principles are unique to NutraSweet. These deserve, and get, more attention in this chapter than the better known concepts.

NutraSweet struggles to apply its organizing concepts just like every other company. Concepts are articulated, experimented with, and rejected when necessary. No one would ever suggest that the company has attained perfection. There are bad, as well as good, experiences from which to learn; NutraSweet is, above all, an active learning system, trying to learn from both.

THE COMPETITIVE WEDGE

To understand what was going on in this company, I found it necessary to organize my thinking through a conceptual model that I call *the competitive wedge*. There are at least eight key design principles in use around NutraSweet, and there are likely others in various stages of discovery and decline. Bob Shapiro, along with several key managers, helped articulate many of these; others I discovered while wandering through the company. Some of these are actively debated internally about their value. What these eight do provide is insight about how the company defines itself and how it goes about its business. There are obvious lessons in these design principles for other companies.

The easiest way to present these eight concepts or principles would be to first list and then explain each of them using examples. A simple listing would, however, ignore their relationship to each other and how they relate to the company's attempt to create sustainable competitive advantage. Instead, the competitive wedge model recognizes their interrelationships. The wedge model is a variation of the contingency models of organization design advocated over the past few years.[4]

The competitive wedge represents the unique configuration of the company's products and services, structure and systems, people, and technologies focused with maximum energy and impact upon the company's chosen markets. Each of these parts of the company can be perfected to provide a basis for competitive advantage, but collectively they provide lasting, maximum impact. The challenge to the company's leadership is to harmoniously integrate each of these "edges" to form a true wedge. The competitive wedge's components are illustrated in Figure 8–1.

FIGURE 8–1
The Competitive Wedge

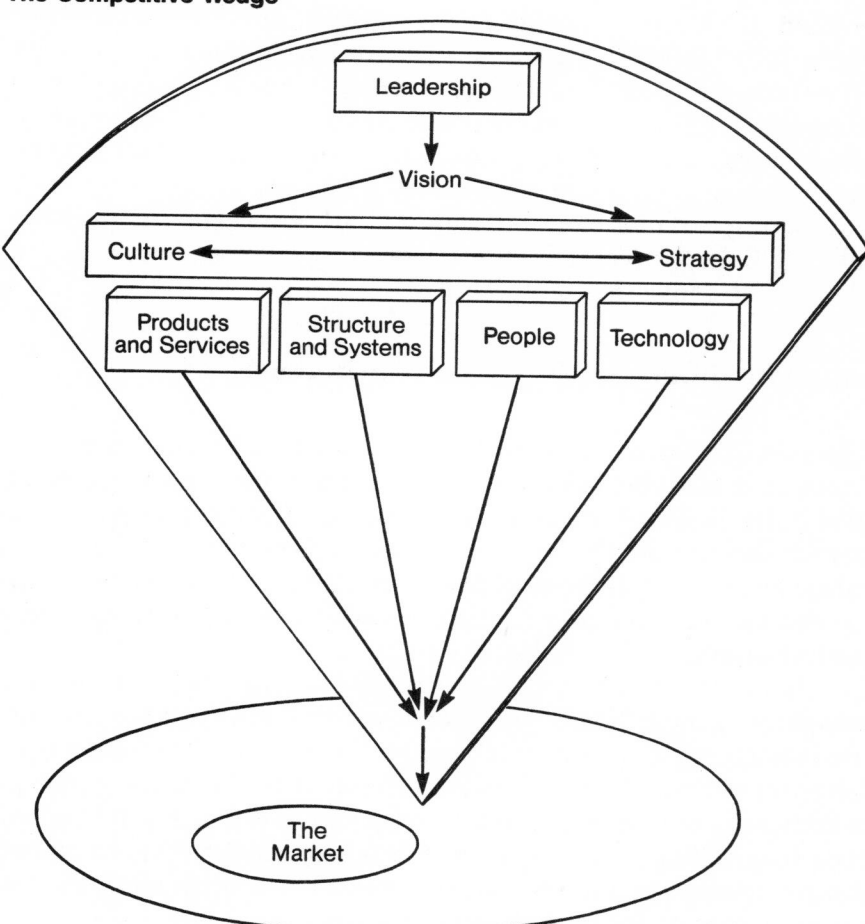

Compete Globally to Succeed Locally

There are three design principles which need to be stated before diving further into this model. The first principle deals with the scope of the markets attacked by the company. For NutraSweet, its basic premise has always been that it must "Compete Globally to Succeed Locally." The company's competitive strategy is inherently global in scope due to the competitive structure of the food industry and scale of opportunities and competitors.

NutraSweet's competitive strategy does not differentiate between domestic and international; such a division is meaningless, if not dangerous. The forceful competitive pressure applied to foreign markets is essential due to the growth potential of those markets, and the ability to keep competitors off-balance within the United States. The lesson for other companies is that they really don't have a competitive strategy these days unless it is global in scope. The domestic U.S. marketplace is large and thus offers some protection for a young innovating company, but only for a short time. The competitive playing field for technology-intensive, innovative companies is global, not domestic.

Innovate, Innovate, Innovate Continuously

The role of innovation is pervasive throughout the wedge model. Innovation must be expressed in each of the model's components to give it the distinctiveness needed to successfully compete with that part of the wedge. The other components are eventually compromised when one is less developed than the others. Indeed, the need for innovation is so strong that NutraSweet's second and even more basic design principle appears to be "Innovate, Innovate, Innovate Continuously." The types of statements that you hear within the company include: "There's no such thing as maturity"; "Don't take anything for granted—nothing is inevitable"; and "Lead out; challenge the organization." There is a sincere curiosity and an ongoing search for ways to improve products and services, technologies, structure and systems, and people. Innovation is a value advanced in the mission statement not just because it sounds nice; it is an absolute competitive necessity.

Preserve a Bias toward Growth

The emphasis upon global scale and continuous innovation reflects a third design principle which Bob Shapiro calls "Preserve a Bias toward Growth." Innovation is dedicated to creating "frontiers" for people to expand into. He notes that "simply doing more of what you're already doing isn't it. You grow into the domain of the unknown to create spaces for something interesting to happen."

Growth gives flexibility and freedom. No growth limits flexibility and choice. It is the biological axiom of "grow or die," whether organizationally or individually, wedded to competitively-driven innovation. Bob knows that he cannot retain the creative talent needed to grow the company if the company doesn't continue to grow. Growth is not necessary just for financial performance reasons. Growth provides the challenge and opportunity for the organization to express its full potential.

BALANCING AND FOCUSING THE WEDGE

The company must not only develop, but must also integrate the components in the competitive wedge to achieve maximum focus and impact. If one of these components is weak, or they are collectively not focused as well as possible, then the wedge is not keen enough to create and sustain competitive advantage in a market. A particularly strong part of the wedge may give temporary advantage, but sustained competitive advantage requires balanced strength across the other wedge parts, as well. It's not exaggerating to say that the competitive wedge is like a spearpoint aimed at a specific market. It has to be as sharp as possible to penetrate deeply. For example, General Motors has invested billions of dollars in advanced manufacturing technologies, yet has apparently still underinvested in other components such as people. As a result, GM may have the most advanced manufacturing technology, but it also has the highest operating costs in the auto industry. The wedge components are still out of balance.

THE LEADER'S ROLE

The challenge to the company's leadership is to harness these components to provide focus and achieve maximum impact. The leader meets this challenge by first defining a vision for the company which best expresses and weds its desired culture (i.e., its operant values and beliefs) with its long-term competitive strategy. Culture and strategy are meshed to bring about the company's vision. The leader, and the focused culture and strategy expressed by the company's vision, represent the spear shaft. They provide the driving force to the wedge components.

There is really very little mystical about defining a vision for a company. The concept of *vision* has received a great deal of attention over the past few years, and the mistake is to separate the vision from the process used in creating it. Defining a vision doesn't just happen; it is the result of a deep, long assessment of the company's competencies, prospects and aspirations, and choices. It thus reflects, to greater or lesser degrees, its members' shared expectations about their company's future. A shared vision is one which sufficiently meshes different sets of expectations to create focused action.

Dr. Egon Zehnder, founder of the largest executive search firm in Europe and a close confidant of many corporate leaders, commented during an interview in Zurich that the leader must be able to relate or interpret the vision from any number of possible perspectives. A vision is potent when it is "multidimensional"; that is, when it can be interpreted and have meaning for all individuals and groups within the organization. It will have meaning and impact only in relation to these individuals and groups.

For NutraSweet, one important expression of its vision is in its Mission Statement (see Appendix B). A revealing sentence in this statement is the first one: "Our Mission is to bring better food choices to consumers through the application of advanced technology." NutraSweet creates desirable food choices by marketing products derived through leading-edge technologies. How the company does this is not defined; the "how" depends upon the company's strategies and culture. Each individual and group within NutraSweet must be able to interpret what that statement means for them, and whether that interpretation meets their expectations and aspirations for the future.

Coming up with the entire statement was hard work. Max Downham and Bob Shapiro traveled around all of the various groups within NutraSweet discussing, debating, and modifying sentences which eventually became part of this statement. It was the result of a collaborative, interactive process spanning more than a year, and it is still subject to interpretation and refinement through ongoing interaction.

Still, the company is a direct reflection of its leader. What Bob Shapiro has been able to do is be an eloquent, consistent interpreter of the company's vision, helping also to lead the debate about its actual operational meaning for the company as business conditions change. As Bob points out, the company's mission is a statement about what the company wants to become, not what it has been. The statement is held up as a challenge, even as a "hypothesis to be explored and tested," as Bob Shapiro once said.[5] While Bob offers his own interpretations of that vision to provide guidance, he leaves it sufficiently ambiguous to preserve room for individual employee interpretation. He advances only a few central themes or common issues at a time to let employees focus their thinking and action. This process, he calls *creating organic resolution*—shared commitment to a limited set of common, central issues that allows decentralized action.

INTENSELY-FOCUSED CULTURES

Getting the sharpest focus to the wedge requires tighter integration between the company's culture and its competitive strategy than perhaps commonly accepted. The relationship between culture and strategy is vague, despite the attention being given to each of them in business books these days.

One view of the relationship between culture and strategy is that choices of strategy are conditioned and confined by the company's culture. Bob Miles, author of *Coffin Nails and Corporate*

Strategy, notes how the strong cultures of the tobacco companies dictated what strategies these companies considered as responses to their increasingly hostile business environment.[6]

On the other hand, the implicit assumption today is that the company's strategy drives its culture. Culture is increasingly seen as a variable changed to support the execution of major shifts in corporate strategy.[7] Jack Welch at GE can set the objective of a business being number one or two in its respective market, but he must also cultivate a culture which values "speed, simplicity, and self-confidence" to help that business objective be achieved.[8] This is done by streamlining work and management systems, encouraging self-expression, and a host of other tangible actions which impact the value and belief systems operating within those businesses. No small feat, but the important point is that culture appears to be serving corporate strategy, not vice versa.

GE and NutraSweet share an important characteristic when it comes to their cultures and strategies. They both have what I call intensely-focused cultures. Neither strategy nor culture totally drives the other; they are actively managed to make sure that they reinforce each other. The values and beliefs inherent in culture are supportive of the company's strategy. Through its execution, the strategy satisfies those values and confirms its beliefs. For example, Mariann Jelinek and Claudia Schoonhoven in their book, *The Innovation Marathon,* note how strategy is pervasive in the cultures of the technology-driven semiconductor companies they studied. In an industry in which costs are routinely driven down 25 percent a year, getting everyone committed to the company's competitive strategy is essential. Strategy, they note, is a common topic and the subject of conversation throughout those companies.[9]

To illustrate this point, NutraSweet's mission statement lists as an important value *courage*—a willingness to challenge the status quo and act on the basis of one's beliefs. In practice, courage is manifested in the company's willingness to challenge food industry norms and compete head-to-head against companies 10 times its size. Strategy and culture serve each other.

The popular view that creative organizations maximize autonomy, individual expression, open experimentation, and prefer egalitarian management simply isn't true in such intensely- focused, innovation-driven, competitive companies like NutraSweet. Effectively balancing and integrating the competitive wedge's core elements requires greater centralization and control by top management than that advocated in earlier, more naive views about creative organizations. The early days at Apple Computer, for example, popularized the view of the young technology company as a loosely-organized, even chaotic but highly creative competitor.[10]

But the competitive stakes risked by today's innovative companies in their global markets are so high that they preclude totally decentralized, autonomous behavior, whether in Apple under John Scully or NutraSweet under Bob Shapiro. NutraSweet is increasingly disciplined about the behaviors which it accepts, but the range of those behaviors is still very broad. Management's task is to encourage some degree of conformity across individuals, groups, and divisions through the sharing of the company's strategy and culture, while still flirting with anarchy. There is a dynamic tension between stability and change that is managed with a strong bias toward change. Order without rigidity is the goal.[11]

The types of controls used in companies with intensely focused cultures vary tremendously from bureaucratic organizations. Bureaucratic control was traditionally achieved through rules, policies, and hierarchies. Control in NutraSweet is sought more through the internalization of the company's basic values and beliefs (i.e., its culture), along with the additional design principles discussed below. There are rules, policies, and hierarchy, but these are recognized as having both pluses and significant minuses; the goal is to maximize their contributions while minimizing their down-side potential. Operationally, what this means is that the prevailing state of affairs and way of doing things is continuously questioned and consciously subverted when it no longer helps execute strategy. It means placing much less emphasis upon formal structures and much more emphasis on the processes that monitor, evaluate, and help make the changes that impact performance. The leader is process designer and manager.

THE PRODUCTS AND SERVICES EDGE

The products and services component in the wedge is concerned with which products are created and how they are supported with customers. If there is anything the NutraSweet story illustrates, it is the inseparability of products and services. The more complex and technology-intensive a product, the more supporting services add value and become essential. A tremendous amount has been written about product and service innovation in the past few years, so this component's dimensions are relatively well-known and will not be reiterated. American companies are catching on to the relationship between products and value-added services provided customers.

The obvious issue in this component for NutraSweet is whether the set of products and services are sufficiently valued by the market to sustain competitive advantage after 1992. The sources of advantage can be price, quality, and level of customer support, whatever the most important dimensions are for a given market. The patent, branded ingredient strategy, perceived high product safety and quality, heavy direct advertising, and customer support had initially helped position aspartame in each of its use markets.

NutraSweet has had little difficulty demonstrating value in either products or services. Price remains the biggest issue; availability is also receding as a long-term issue as capacity is added over the next three years. However, whether its customer support services for aspartame after 1992 will continue to be valued is a concern. The intimate relationship created with customers through the regulatory and product-testing process has already demonstrated that customers do value these services. The question is rather whether the company has, in effect, simply educated and prepared the market for generic aspartame after 1992. Its largest customers may well not need the close support needed for new applications; for them, the biggest issue will be price. Whether Simplesse will have penetrated the market deeply enough to replace the revenue slack which could result is a corollary question.

NutraSweet's value-added services for adopters may have been most appropriate for an earlier stage of the market. What new services customers will value are less clear, yet the prospect of competing on price and quality alone is unlikely. As baked goods applications for aspartame become feasible, another wave of value-added, customer support is already beginning. The Simplesse strategy is the same, except with the wrinkle that the company appears very willing to introduce food products of its own directly into the market.

The interaction between strategy, company culture, and products and services is complex, but obvious. For NutraSweet, the aggressive marketing of aspartame, and unorthodox dual marketing channel strategy for Simplesse, illustrates how the company's culture is reflected in its products and services. Testing and rejecting traditional food industry practices, for example, is a direct reflection of the company's culture, and it does so with its command of pharmaceutical-industry scientific standards and an understanding of the regulatory process.

More problematic is the challenge of becoming and staying the low-cost producer of aspartame when the culture has been oriented more toward start-ups and new product innovation. Here, Monsanto plays a critical role. The company's traditional values are now in transition to meet the shift in strategy. The shift is confined to only the NutraSweet group, however, since Simplesse and Business Ventures are not, and should not be, adopting a low-cost producer strategy and culture. There is, of course, tremendous room within the NutraSweet group for process innovation and product extensions into new geographic markets.

THE STRUCTURE AND SYSTEMS EDGE

The reorganization of the company in 1988 was recognition that the company had arrived at several points in its life all at once. That is, issues found with more mature companies were coexisting with issues related to new product innovation. It was clear that a more robust structure and systems were needed to organize these issues. In every instance, however, the goal has been to keep structure and systems lean, simple, and as uncluttered as possible. It takes tremendous creativity to prevent hardening of the arteries, which naturally begins to set in with greater size and complexity. For example, a cost accounting system should be adopted which monitors the value added by each activity within the company; value-added cost accounting systems are, however, still in their infancy. The temptation is to use one which really doesn't supply the information needed for innovation-intensive companies. The systems dictate what becomes possible.

To preserve flexibility while providing structure, NutraSweet uses three absolutely critical design principles. I think of these almost as general mandates that ask all employees to "Work against Boundaries," "Create, Not Just React, to the Environment," and "Nurture Self-Designing Behavior." In a sense, these design principles sprang from Bob Shapiro and many managers' early negative experiences in highly structured, bureaucratic organizations. For Shapiro, his early experiences included a stint in government positions that allowed him to witness naive attempts by urban planners to rebuild cities and neighborhoods. The planners overcontrolled and overcentralized the process, and the resulting building and housing complexes were social and economic disasters.

Work against Boundaries

"Work against Boundaries" literally means accepting the need for a minimal amount of structure between work units and hierarchical levels, while always understanding the negative consequences of the mental and operational boundaries which emerge. Boundaries, like those found in a living cell, serve a function; they buffer the internal functions from external disturbances and provide identity to the organism. But boundaries need to be highly permeable to let information flow. The task within NutraSweet is to allow sufficient boundaries to give individuals and work groups an identity, but to keep them focused outward, not inward. It means creating a culture built around collaboration and cooperation to manage shared issues and challenges. Restated, the goal is to organize around issues, as well as tasks. There is, of course, an organization chart which shows groups organized around core tasks and products, but the organization chart does not show the incessant interaction that occurs around issues which cut across these groups.

There is also a metaphysical aspect to this design principle, something consistently true about whatever Shapiro asserts. Boundaries don't simply refer to organizational boundaries, but also to mental boundaries. The admonition is to test limits and the way problems and choices are framed. "What is The Nu- traSweet Company?" is not just a rhetorical question, but one asked seriously and often around the company. The reframing of the company's scope from being an artificial sweetener company to a sugar replacement company, and now, with Simplesse, a technology-intensive, health-oriented food company illustrates this principle in practice.

There is also a level of irreverence tolerated in the company that many CEOs would find uncomfortable. The "tomato poster" is a classic example. Bob Shapiro wanted to invite comments from employees, both supportive and negative, and allowed a poster of himself to be created that showed a big orange tomato splashed across part of the poster with the inscription "Give Me Your Best Shot." The poster was meant to symbolize that no one is to be idolized or set apart from others in the organization. Hierarchy has a func- tion, but it shouldn't ever come to create boundaries between em- ployees that prevented candid, direct communication.

Rather than create confusion—some of which is desirable, anyway—the idea is to create an openness to new ways of doing things. The branded ingredient strategy, the bootstrapping of the Harbor Beach hybrid process, the 100 percent NutraSweet labeling strategy for soft drinks, possible dual-channel market- ing strategy for Simplesse, and Desserve Cafes are additional examples of ways conventional conceptions of the food industry were challenged.

"Create, Not Just React, to the Environment"

A corollary design principle also employed to free-up thinking was demonstrated in NutraSweet even earlier than the above examples. Don Rumsfeld and John Robson were firmly commit- ted to the idea that the company had to "Create, Not Just React, to the Environment." The unheard of, and fortunately unnecessary, strategy of suing the FDA to break the approval stalemate in 1981, coupled with the successful "one-legged Hopi" amendment effort that extended the patent's life, are two examples of how Searle chose to create, not just react, to its environment. It means proactively engaging the environment to shape conditions and forces before they impact the company.

NutraSweet learned the need for more proactive management of its environment the hard way. The regulatory debacle demonstrated the need to develop a more sophisticated internal government, consumer, and legal affairs management capacity. The company has begun sponsoring industry conferences about food industry issues and continues funding ongoing clinical studies of its products to make sure it stays out in front of issues. By challenging its environment, NutraSweet demonstrates the fundamental competitive advantage which proactive companies gain; they get to set everyone else's agenda.

Nurture Self-Designing Behavior

"Nurture Self-Designing Behavior" is closely related to the boundaries and proactive principles because it, too, encourages employees to "create opportunity space" except at their own job and work group levels. It also apparently applies even to the business level. Rob Kazanjian, an Emory professor, and I were trying to figure out just what we had heard after a two-day trip to Deerfield early in 1989, when Rob made the observation that people were apparently being asked to "design themselves"—the "selves" were being asked to design their own jobs.

The traditional design process used by an organization centers around the division and grouping of tasks and activities based on their interdependencies with each other into jobs and work groups. The organization's technology, distribution of power and resources, and a number of other factors influence the division of labor which occurs. Conversely, self-designing behavior springs from the individual and group's capacities and motivation for assuming greater responsibility and authority. The desire is to expand job scope by making tasks more whole and integrated.

While it is certainly essential to group tasks together which make most sense, the tendency in bureaucracies is to create job positions and work groups on the basis of a smaller (not larger) set of activities to be performed. A level of responsibility and authority is assigned to a job and group which minimizes its impact on performance if tasks are not performed. It is an ageless game of dividing and redividing tasks and activities that are, in fact, fundamentally whole. As Bob Shapiro said about the typical bureaucratic approach, "You end up dividing jobs so small that you only get small people. They never have a picture of the whole." Over time, people tend to become what their job descriptions say.

As a solution, Bob's strategy is to keep jobs as large as possible to force people to exercise judgment and recognize priorities. Rather than simply hire more market researchers to perform the company's market research internally, external market research firms are used to keep a fewer number of internal staff responsible and capable of appreciating and managing the entire market research activity. Doing so makes economic sense, as well, but the more basic motivation is to keep people focused on larger priorities and issues, not managing a legion of staff. You can manage issues and priorities or you can manage the structure you create. It is a question of focus, once again.

The basic goal is to expand job scope as much as possible for individuals and for groups. Employees are encouraged to enlarge their "circle of responsibility and authority" to the greatest extent they believe possible. This process has been called *empowering* by a number of writers.[12] The assumption is that people want responsibility and can handle it. An inability to give it creates morale and turnover problems, and employees who can't grow into positions of greater authority over time. This possibility helps explain some of the conflict between NutraSweet's corporate level and the "unruly kids" in Augusta. Empowering people also assumes that they, like their company, are in the "process of becoming"—of growing and changing— and narrow job scopes confine both them and the company which must depend upon their growth for its future.

The big question is how can you empower individuals and groups while still controlling their performance? When has the circle of responsibility and authority expanded too far? The goal should be to let job scope expand up to the point that it is productive to do so. There is no tangible rule or point for knowing when that point has been reached. The danger, of course, is that the individual or group becomes overloaded and makes mistakes and burns-out. Confusion about responsibilities can also increase and activities fall through the cracks.

The answers to these questions are not obvious. Two of the early key managers in Augusta, Ralph Bietz and Dave Sharp, agreed that empowering people requires as a prerequisite a tremendously self-confident leader. It then requires time and experience with the individual, and trust. Active, multidirectional flows of communication and effective teamwork are essential for trust.

What is trust, after all? It means that people behave in consistent ways; that they don't have to question each others' motives, as Max Downham once suggested, and that they do not act from self-interest alone. It also means in a work setting that risk-taking is encouraged and rewarded, not punished. If someone reaches out and enlarges their "circle" by voluntarily taking on additional responsibilities, and then makes a mistake, the company's response becomes a crucial indicator of trust.

Trust is a concept I encountered more than once in NutraSweet and several other very innovation-intensive companies. What has become clear is that leading-edge companies like NutraSweet feel very comfortable using soft, squishy concepts like trust as a way of managing. Recall from the last chapter the shift that was described from "machine age to organic, systems thinking." Physical models of the organization using hierarchy and structure are giving way to more organic, even spiritually-based models of organization that emphasize values and beliefs.

Trust is therefore not just an *outcome* of managing, but a *way* of managing. It is used in place of rules and hierarchy. These concepts are extremely difficult for rational organization designers to accept because they are qualitative and hard to operationalize. Designers get uncomfortable when they don't know how to measure and replicate concepts in other organizations. Nonetheless, managers like Bietz, Sharp and Downham find "soft" concepts like trust essential for managing a complex, rapidly changing work environment. These concepts provide the basis for empowering people and groups so that they may voluntarily fill the spaces created by growth and change. They build commitment and provoke creativity.

At a business level, self-designing behavior means that no two businesses should be designed and operated the same way if they spring from different technologies and are targeted against different markets. Perhaps this sounds overly obvious. The point is that tremendous flexibility is needed in designing a new business. There shouldn't be a cookie-cutter approach to growing businesses that imposes a "one best way" solution on the new business.

Within NutraSweet, the technology and market conditions that Simplesse represented were fundamentally different from aspartame. Simplesse was rightly recognized as a separate business, not just another product in a product line to be managed with a prevailing organization design. The goal is to let Simplesse as a division emerge and unfold based upon its inherent differences and potential. Within the seed is the latent company. A great many new businesses created within today's largest, most well-known companies smother their new born by inappropriately imposing structure and processes.

THE PEOPLE EDGE

It's an understatement to say that the type and skills of the people within the company are central to its success. They must be willing and able to accept responsibility and manage the inherent, often overwhelming, ambiguity that is present. It should be very clear, then, that the way NutraSweet and other intensely-focused companies like it design themselves can be incredibly hard on people. I don't mean that they are cruel and inhumane, of course. Instead, I mean that there is perhaps nothing more important in the company than the selection, development, and separation processes used. The company and employees both live at the edge of their capabilities.

What this style of life means is that you have to find, develop, and retain the best people possible. Within NutraSweet resides one of the largest, deepest "gene pools" of management and scientific talent within the industry. Providing the resources to develop this pool, and the right incentives to retain its members, is one of the most important challenges presently within the company. For a company that's familiar with advanced bio-technology, the metaphor of "developing the gene pool" isn't surprising. The competitive sports metaphor also internally kicked around refers to this task as "developing an All-Star team." The people component in NutraSweet's competitive wedge is equal, if not more important, than the other components in that model.

There was an early attempt at selecting employees for the right attitude, not just skills, when the NutraSweet division was first formed. A trace of animosity still lingers between employees in Searle and NutraSweet due to that early selection process. Some of the traits sought were hard to quantify, such as flexibility, entrepreneurial spirit, ability to handle uncertainty, and so forth. These were particularly important traits at the plant level because all were start-up situations.

Whether these same traits are as important now in some parts of the company is a question asked at several points in this book. As the need for different types of employees becomes clear, and other employees can no longer grow to meet the demands being created, a very difficult area for work becomes creating a separation policy which minimizes both harm and guilt to the individual and to the company.

There have been, of course, hundreds of thousands of jobs cut from companies going through down-sizing and restructuring over the past decade, but you have to realize how traumatic the exceptionally small number of separations are for younger, smaller innovative companies like NutraSweet. Painful doesn't describe the feeling I sensed when talking with NutraSweet managers about incidents which required the separation of an employee or manager from the company. When Bob Shapiro talks about a humane, guilt-free separation policy being the most difficult area for innovative thinking, he means it. Bob Shapiro once remarked, "I never wanted to manage people; I wanted colleagues."

Because people are so critical to success, note how many of the design principles described so far relate to people, not just markets or company structure. Principles such as "Nurture Self-Designing Behavior," for example, not only assure that work will be performed effectively, but that the people performing the work will be challenged and given room for growth. The goal has been to create a culture and a climate which appeals to people's minds and hearts. Given the competitive pressures the company now faces, Shapiro deeply believes that, "We can win only if there are people who are prepared to fight for this company. They have to see something worth fighting for to make this happen." That is the essence of the people component in NutraSweet.

THE TECHNOLOGY EDGE

The last component in the competitive wedge model refers to more than the tangible process technology of the company. It includes the entire knowledge and skill base of the company, as well, and these reside within employees. The technology edge reflects the collective know-how the company can bring to bear both at a point in time and over time. With this definition in mind, the technology component is particularly strong in NutraSweet. The company works ceaselessly in making sure it has achieved competitive advantage with respect to its hard and soft technologies.

A great deal of attention has been focused on competitive advantage recently by technology-intensive American companies. In the case of some technologies such as semiconductors, competitive advantage may well have been lost.[13] In other industries like bio-technology, the Japanese are trying to gain position, but American companies are still in dominant positions. How the United States can preserve (even rebuild) advantage is *the* question, and the prescriptions run the gamut of improving quality, service, manufacturing productivity, and designing creative organization structures and management practices. Obviously, initiatives in all of these areas are important.

Without question, NutraSweet's pharmaceutical heritage is a major asset in creating and preserving its market position. The

R&D activities within Mike Losee's Technology and Development Group are disciplined, well-funded, and professionally staffed. The process technologies within the company are supported not only with Losee's staff, but with experienced Nutra-Sweet technicians and Monsanto engineers with strong biotechnology and continuous process technology backgrounds. There is no other comparable company in the U.S. food industry. Then there is Ajinomoto, both as an ally and as a model.

Embrace Your Technology

It is worth reiterating that a competitive edge in technology was never assured for NutraSweet. Indeed, back at the beginning Searle had almost lost the use patent for aspartame to Ajinomoto. Searle was later still totally dependent upon Ajinomoto until the bootlegged Harbor Beach fermentation experiment. Harbor Beach demonstrated the ability of Searle to actually innovate in large scale fermentation process technology, and paved the way for funding future experiments that have given NutraSweet a major technological advantage.

While Ajinomoto technology, and later Monsanto technology, provided a solid foundation for NutraSweet, the lesson has been made clearly and forcefully: regain control of your future by regaining control of your technology. The new imperative within NutraSweet is "Don't Just Accept, Embrace Your Technology." Where some companies would license away their technologies, NutraSweet is totally convinced that its future success depends upon its ability to master its technology and control it, even regain control if control had been lost. It literally means not just knowing your technology, but knowing it like no other company.

A company can dominate a market with its command of the relevant technologies used to compete in that market. The company needs to have more than what is increasingly called a "technology strategy." The "strategic use of technology", to use a concept offered by Joseph Morone in his 1989 *California Management Review* article, "Strategic Use of Technology", means that technology is integral to strategy, even that technology shapes strategy.[14] He contends:

What distinguishes the innovative firm is not just that it is more efficient in applying technology to meet its ends (i.e., in technology strategy), but that its ends are themselves shaped by technology. Technology creates strategic opportunities; innovative companies recognize these opportunities and build corporate strategy around them.

NutraSweet has used its technology strategically both with aspartame and with Simplesse. But it has done so creatively, and that makes a big, big difference. Aspartame became NutraSweet brand aspartame, the first branded ingredient in food industry history. Simplesse is another branded ingredient which can be marketed through multiple marketing channels. The company has wisely invested in its technology edge and understands its strategic importance in market applications.

DESIGNING AN INNOVATING COMPANY— A SUMMARY

This chapter's basic premise is that innovating firms are characterized by the design principles they use to compete in their chosen markets. The principles serve as governing assumptions and ground rules for directing the attention, energies, and resources of the company to that end. The competitive wedge model is a simple way of expressing the need for focusing the critical parts of the company to achieve maximum impact in a chosen market. An important aspect of this model is the need to not just develop one or two components, but all of them. Development needs to be balanced because they are so interdependent with each other. A company can stumble onto a great product and gain initial market success, but that success will be short-lived if the other components in the wedge are not rapidly developed and brought into balance. Successful, sustained competitive advantage accrues to those companies that work ceaselessly to create balance and articulate design principles to guide them in this process. NutraSweet knows this fact of life.

A great many issues are left unresolved for the company, its industry, and for technology-intensive, innovating companies in general. The final chapter poses these challenges.

CHAPTER 9

UNRESOLVED CHALLENGES

One hundred years ago, drugs were where food is today.
—*Bob Shapiro*

Up to this point we've had a close look at the evolution of The NutraSweet Company from its roots within G. D. Searle & Co., through the regulatory struggle and manufacturing start-up, and up to the present where it is trying to quickly position itself for the future. The NutraSweet story is also valuable because it is a vehicle for discussing many of the forces at work that are impacting innovative companies. Over the course of NutraSweet's evolution, the global competitive economy as a playing field for innovation has undergone fundamental changes. NutraSweet has tried to articulate creative principles for building its competitive wedge in its markets. Whether it has done so effectively enough to double and triple its size and maintain its stellar performance is an excellent question only the future can answer. Personally, I think the company has a lot going for it.

Sweet Success raises a number of tangential issues in the process of telling NutraSweet's story. These issues are important enough to deserve confronting in this last chapter. They pose major challenges for consumers and companies operating within the food industry, and for government policy makers more generally.

FOOD INDUSTRY CHALLENGES

At a food industry level, Bob Shapiro's quote opening this chapter illustrates the impact technologically sophisticated, highly innovative companies want to have, and likely will have, upon the way all of us relate to food. The entry of such companies into this industry is the equivalent of the emergence of bio-engineering in the pharmaceutical industry.

This trend is welcomed within the food industry because from nearly every perspective, this industry is mature and therefore offering limited growth prospects for giants like Kraft, Procter & Gamble, and General Mills. Understand, of course, that their markets aren't disappearing; it's just that they aren't growing rapidly. The processed food industry is a $230 billion market which experienced a number of positive trends in the 1980s. The 1990s aren't as promising as these trends now tail-away or reverse.[1] For example, industry restructurings and mergers contributed to improved margins and sales growth, but both of these trends will likely diminish.

Many of the innovations finding their way into this industry are in the treating and packaging of foods to improve their shelf life and convenience.[2] "Food engineering" of the sort that gives micro-waved food a texture closer to oven-baked foods is useful, but limited in its economic contribution or impact on the market position of the company. Much of the new-and-improved food products coming to the market therefore represent essentially incremental and marginal innovations. Crunchier microwaved lasagna may be nice, but it isn't going to destabilize anyone's entrenched market position. The advertising agencies do well, I guess.

Probably one of the most important trends to come along in the past decade, with no end in sight, is the increase awareness of consumers about their health and nutrition. The soft-drink companies understand this trend well, as pointed out in Chapter 5. The diet brand segment is forecast to be nearly 50 percent of the market by the end of the decade.

Launching innovative new products into this wave promises faster growth and an opportunity to destabilize the balance of power among the industry giants. NutraSweet's success has obviously been observed with great interest by a great many domestic and international food and chemical companies. However, in the process of seizing opportunities posed by this new health and nutrition consciousness, many of the food companies have stumbled all over themselves.

The Price of Confusion

In reality, we are now totally confused about our health and nutrition. Bob Shapiro once said in a conversation, "We are now in a problematic relationship with our food—can we trust it? We also expect more from our food." This situation is a tremendous challenge for companies like NutraSweet, because the confusion is creating both market opportunities as well as a monumental risk that consumers will react negatively to health and diet claims from the food companies. And confusion can lead to increased government regulation and consumer movement away from foods making such claims.

In a 1989 *Wall Street Journal* sponsored survey of American consumers' concerns about food and nutrition, consumers were found to be schizophrenic about their diets, often reverting back from so-called healthy foods to foods that were neither healthy nor nutritious.[3] The reversion is due to stress, habit, and social pressures ("Oh come on, just one more little piece"). The introduction of low calorie foods also lets us play games like: "Well, I had a Diet Coke, so I guess I can now have that chocolate cake." Whether low calorie sweeteners or fats will dramatically reduce consumption of sugar and fat is less than certain; the relationship is likely not one-for-one. Perhaps a 20 percent increase in the consumption of low fat foods will reduce overall fat consumption by 15 percent.

The food companies have a notorious history of not helping clarify health and diet issues for consumers. The FDA is an institutional solution to a social problem that has been around for decades. While blatant abuse by food companies is rare these days, the food companies' advertising and labeling practices are still under scrutiny for good reasons. Procter and Gamble, for example, challenged General Mills in 1989 for introducing its Benefit brand cereal, a product that P&G felt was a drug packaged and advertised as a food. General Mills argued that the cereal reduced cholesterol, and did so in part due to its high fiber content. So much fiber that Benefit's label read:

> Gradually increase amount. We suggest starting with one-half serving of Benefit and gradually increasing to a full serving. Always consume Benefit with milk. If digestive discomfort occurs, consult a physician and avoid laxatives. Children should limit consumption to one serving per day.[4]

Is this a food or a drug? That's what Procter & Gamble and General Mills are arguing about. The line between the pharmaceutical and food industries is getting fuzzier. More recently, remember oat bran? To the defense of the food companies, the whole area of nutrition and health is extremely complex, with many, many unanswered questions. Contrary results from scientifically rigorous studies are common, almost anticipated. Keep in mind the discussion of "science as a moving target" in a previous chapter. Science is relative, as well as absolute.

Many nonengineered foods are surrounded by as many misconceptions as more complex products like aspartame. Take sugar, for example. Are honey and brown sugar more nutritious for you than white sugar? If you grew up in California in the 1960s shopping in health food stores like I did, the answer is obvious, right? Wrong. Sugar is sugar.

Maybe everyone is confused about health and nutrition claims, yet the food companies have certainly exacerbated the problem. As a consequence, confidence in the food industry is low. In a 1989 *Washington Post* poll of consumers, only 3 percent believed that food manufacturers never made misleading claims about the health benefits of their products; a third of the respondents in this survey said they made "a lot" of misleading claims.[5] The concerns are real enough that federal guidelines are being introduced to remove some of the confusion.[6]

The challenge for NutraSweet is to communicate clearly and convincingly about its products, and differentiate itself as much as possible from other food companies. The company tries to do this, spending millions of dollars in direct advertising (two ads on the radio even as I was typing the first draft of this chapter—no exaggeration!), and presenting itself as a concerned, scientifically-based company involved in society. These activities are honestly performed because the company is committed to its mission statement. If you're a diabetic, there is also little question that NutraSweet has improved your life. But the anecdotal, scientifically-unsupported stories still surface about headaches caused by drinking diet soft drinks.[7] The element of doubt remains, and it is increasingly clear that the distrust consumers have for their food is being carried over to specific products. Bob Shapiro's comment about the problematic relationship we now have with food is unfortunately accurate.

This is a company problem. The challenge is to inspire trust and confidence in a company's products, something no food company has consistently and explicitly attempted as part of its strategy to any remarkable and memorable extent.

This is also an industry problem. The challenge here is for the numerous industry associations to pick up the debate and focus discussion among companies to establish ground rules and guidelines without government intervention. It is likely too late for self-regulation. The industry is shooting itself in the foot by contributing to the problem of confused consumers concerned about their nutrition and health.

The Cumulative Impact of Good Ideas

As the number of truly innovative food additives grows, whether as sugar, fat, or salt substitutes, their cumulative impact on the nutrition and health of consumers also grows. Any single product, aspartame for example, may be a welcomed addition to the food supply. Americans, in general, need fewer calories. Add to aspartame the coming set of fat substitutes like Simplesse. Together they make an intriguing combination; low fat, low calorie cheesecake is something to truly look forward to.

Add to these additives several others already here and yet to come. Each product in itself is a useful one; together they present new challenges for regulators, food companies, researchers, and consumers. Part of the concern is that these engineered foods will "shoulder out" more nutritious, healthy foods.[8] A related issue is whether other valuable nutrients are lost in the process of creating an "engineered" food. For example, food companies are supplementing their breads with additional fibers not normally part of the food. The fear is that these high-fiber brands may potentially reduce the absorption of other nutrients in the food, while also doing positive things like reducing cholesterol. Replacing fat in our diet is not a bad idea, but the trick is to make sure a nutritious, healthy balance between foods is achieved. Achieving a healthy balance has, of course, been a goal even without calorie and fat substitutes.

A third issue is concerned about the cumulative impact of an entire diet that may become composed of supplemented and altered foods. Estimates are that as much as 30 to 60 percent of all food products containing fat will be impacted by fat substitutes.[9] That's a sizable range, but at even the low end an amazingly large number.

This issue is still at the edge of our thinking. There is very little research looking at the cumulative impact of additives and supplements. At a company-level, aspartame and Simplesse are important innovations. Yet the company can do little to impact the total volume of food products of all kinds in the food supply using additives, substitutes, and supplements.

At an industry and societal level, it is clear that we need to better appreciate the cumulative impact of these products, and make sure that consumers are educated enough to make informed choices. This has always been a challenge, but the scope and nature of the challenge is changing.

SOCIETAL CHALLENGES

After about two years of studying The NutraSweet Company, and a few more years of researching other technology-intensive companies, two major challenges stand clearly in the way of our evolution into the most technologically advanced, competitive nation in the world. First, our global competitiveness in several important industries is slipping away. Second, the benefits of technological advancement are being unevenly distributed across our society. There is a growing gap between those that create technology, those that use it productively in their companies and personal lives, and those that are simply used by technology.

Achieving Global Competitive Advantage

One of the greatest ironies of this book is that it was almost a story about how another American company lost out to a Japanese company for another new product. Ajinomoto almost got to the patent office before Searle to apply for the use patent on aspartame. Although Searle got the patent, NutraSweet to this day utilizes some aspects of Ajinomoto's process technology to produce aspartame. If it wasn't for the gutsy decision to develop an innovative alternate process technology, the dependency would be much more pronounced. The relationship would have been so one-sided that the patent expiration in 1992 would effectively mean the end of NutraSweet's place in the market.

But that's not what happened, of course, and NutraSweet is very much in the sweetener market and poised to enter other food industry segments. The lesson driven home in *Sweet Success* is that American firms need to jealously guard their technology and master it so completely that it becomes a major source of sustainable competitive advantage. Alliances and joint ventures are disarmingly attractive. They can be nothing more than a mortgage on the future, in reality. If necessary, companies need to regain control over their technology if they've lost it.

The company needs a technology strategy—a strategy for developing and employing its know-how and skills as part of its larger competitive strategy. Even more, the technology edge, as it was called in Chapter 8, must be integrated and balanced with the other parts of the competitive wedge. The company's culture and strategy, from a technology perspective, must be focused so keenly that the company's technology is central, and technological innovation becomes an expectation that is nurtured with dedication. As Harold Edmondson and Steven Wheelwright said in a 1989 *California Management Review* article:

> . . . as new product technologies have demanded tighter, more-precise manufacturing tolerances, firms have discovered that manufacturing science must evolve and progress at a rate commensurate with product science, to realize commercially viable applications through new products and new processes.[10]

Technological innovation has to be manifested in all parts of the company (not just plants) if products and services are to reflect the company's full competitive potential. A commitment to innovation and technology means sophisticated data bases in marketing for market research, flexible and responsive computer and information systems, and unquestioned support for R&D at a level well above industry averages. It means responsive accounting and financial reporting systems that better reflect value-added contributions by the parts of the company. It means a great many choices being made daily in favor of competing through innovation.

For the United States, we must begin idolizing the manufacturing manager and scientist, much less the deal maker and corporate development staffer. Idolizing is perhaps too strong a word, but the idea is that the action is in the operations of the company, not at the investment banker's offices on Wall Street. Ivy-league MBAs need to see manufacturing as an attractive personal challenge and a viable career path. Will our society again honor and reward the manufacturing line manager as deserved?

Contrast this approach to a joint-venture strategy. Rather than build a distribution network, you access someone else's. The advantage is that it is likely cheaper and quicker. The disadvantage is that it isn't yours. You gain less in experience and knowledge when you use someone else's.

For the actively acquisitive firm, the relatively large incremental revenue increases that appear step-wise with each acquisition require successively larger deals to be executed since the denominator gets bigger each time. Acquisitions can be extremely useful for gaining entry to a new market or technology, but the danger is that the active acquirer never develops, or impoverishes, the capacity for internal innovation.

The company can't go it alone, however. The abuses of mergers and acquisitions, and the willingness to license away a new technology have roots in government policies and the financial community. Liberal accounting practices, which encouraged the use of excessive leverage, fueled a significant portion of the most recent merger and acquisition wave.

Changes in tax policy also fueled an explosion of venture capital money in the 1970s and early 1980s, which has now moved from early-stage seed and start-up equity investments in high technology industries to later-stage, debt-based buyouts in low technology industries. So who is supplying the early stage money needed to fund new technology start-ups? Corporations, many of them foreign, and of those many are Japanese.

There are plenty of prescriptions for how government can play a meaningful role in reestablishing and building American competitiveness. Using the Japanese experience as a model, some authors like Ira Magaziner and Robert Reich advocate industrial policy for targeted industries, while other researchers advocate more open market responses.[11]

One way that government could certainly help companies is to streamline the regulatory process to prevent drawn-out sagas of the incredibly time and resource-consuming kind NutraSweet experienced. Some of the difficulty was caused by Searle, the company's executives would readily admit. Much of it wasn't the company's fault, however. Congress agreed. It was only through John Robson's creative "one-legged Hopi amendment" strategy that the company got sufficient time to develop a market position before the patent lapses.

The tragedy is that there is absolutely nothing to prevent a similar drawn-out process from reoccurring. Products need to come to market quickly enough to allow companies to establish positions and recapture their investments. On the other hand, the FDA is torn by the need to protect consumers, and a too hasty approval can cause tremendous damage. This is the dilemma: how to support innovation by managing a responsive regulatory process without compromising the health and safety of consumers. Can agencies like the FDA be effective and satisfy all of their stakeholders, or must they make trade-offs that work to the disadvantage of one or another of its constituents? In a global economy crowded with powerful competitors, working frequently hand-in-hand with their governments, this question needs more attention than it has been given.

The "Public Perception of Science"

I want to close *Sweet Success* with a statement of personal concern that technology-intensive companies generally do not appreciate their collective impact on society. There are many unique CEOs who have the historical perspective and intellectual intensity to understand how their products and services are altering society. Bob Shapiro is one of these. Still, most companies continue to flood the markets and society with new technology, often before a previous technology was effectively absorbed. The three-way, dynamic tension among culture, government, and technology described in Chapter 7 is more disturbed than ever.

A reader could be convinced at this point that I am in reality a closet Luddite—a person who is antitechnology. Far from the case, technology, and the constant process of technological innovation, are most likely also our salvation from major problems like environmental pollution. My concern has to do with the uneven distribution and impact of technology within the society. Take communications technology, as an example. A 1990 report from the Office of Technology Assessment to Congress titled "Critical Connections: Communications for the Future" stated, among many things, that the concept of universal telephone service on a common, shared network is breaking down.[12] A two-tiered system is evolving: one private and one public. Government has a role in this specific case due to regulatory restrictions and taxation policies on media owners.

Computer technology is another example. Playing video games is one form of use, but programming the software to run the games is another use. One person is a user, the other the controller. Using computers to gain competitive advantage over another individual, group, or organization is instinctual; tools are used for those purposes in a free, capitalistic society. Providing access to everyone on an equal basis to acquire the skills to compete with computer technology is a political issue. The politics of technology are going to be squarely facing us in the 1990s.

There is an emerging class-system built around access and command over technology. There are the "owners" who created and command the technology because they know its sources and dimensions. This class reaps the greatest gains and clearly wields tremendous power and influence. There are the "users" who understand a technology and can apply it productively to their advantage. There are the "abusers" who do not understand the technology, but are exposed to it and use it in limited ways. This class will go along for the ride on a new technology, whether it is to their betterment or not. Then there are the "outsiders" who literally remain outside the realm of technology, feel great discomfort around it, and avoid it to the extent possible.

Membership in one or another of these classes has direct economic and political impact for the individual and for society as a whole. It is an unpleasant scenario that conjures visions of a technocracy, not a democracy. Given the deteriorating state of American public education, my concern is that we are producing larger numbers of abusers and outsider classes. Technology can help improve one's life; technology can also victimize. Something can be new, and not better. The threat arises from the outsiders who can negatively react to technology, even though they do not understand it.

Clearly, the challenge is to better understand how to communicate about complex science. NutraSweet's Gerry Gaull believes that this issue has to do with what he calls "the public perception of science." If NutraSweet is to introduce innovative new food products into the world's food supply, then it must be able to clearly and convincingly communicate with its "publics" (consumers, regulators, etc.) about those products. Maybe people will simply consume the products without questioning; there fortunately is a very big users group. In some ways a company must certainly hope that it has consumers who simply accept their product without question. The danger is, however, that concerns about health and safety are beginning to dominate consumer thinking, and a company may not be able to allay those fears.

Companies are going to have to learn how to communicate effectively about technologies that most consumers do not understand. On the one hand, they can simply decide not to inform consumers about what they are doing with their technologies because consumers will only get confused and concerned. On the other hand, they can tell consumers about their technologies, hopefully in a way to help consumers use the product or service productively and to inspire their confidence.

How can you do this? This is a very difficult question, and companies do better and worse in finding their own answer. For example, NutraSweet provides toll-free phone numbers for consumers to receive information and voice concerns, a common practice these days. A number of other methods are also employed, yet the challenge remains formidable. My point is that it is going to become an even greater challenge.

Take the bio-technology industry as an example. Here is an incredibly promising technological area for endless innovation, but it can also conjure up our most basic fears and bad dreams. The negative reaction to bio-technology over the past decade has slowed a great many new product introductions in animal science, agriculture, and human health.

I am certainly not advocating introducing drugs or hybrid life forms without rigorous testing, but the point I want to make is that many of the bio-technology companies involved were unable to communicate clearly and convincingly about their technologies. With an imperfect track record for effectively regulating new technologies, government agencies have legitimacy difficulties of their own. Witness the nuclear energy industry and the sadly compromised roles of the NRA and EPA. A sophisticated adversary like Jeremy Rifkin, who not only understands the law but how to use an often hyperactive media, can block not only an introduction, but even the testing of an innovative product for years.[13]

So, the technology-intensive company that wants to continue innovating in a society taking on these dimensions has some critical new skills to develop. It must become an excellent communicator and able to engage a less-than-informed society in a dialogue about what it is doing. With the number of exceptional, unfortunate screw-ups finding welcome attention by the media, the climate is clearly getting tricky for a company of this type. NutraSweet has learned a great deal, and continues to learn as it competes on the global competitive playing field for innovation it has chosen. Its world has changed a lot since James Schlatter licked his finger that day.

ENDNOTES

CHAPTER 1

1. Steven P. Schnaars. *Megamistakes: Forecasting and the Myth of Rapid Technological Change*. New York: Free Press, 1989.
2. Robert B. Shapiro. "Security Analyst Presentation." New York, N.Y., March 18, 1986. Copy available from The NutraSweet Company.
3. Shapiro. "Security Analyst Presentation."
4. Roger Enrico and Jesse Kornbluth. *The Other Guy Blinked*. New York: Bantam Books, 1986, p. 72.
5. Michael E. Porter. *Competitive Advantage*. New York: Free Press, 1985, p. 109.
6. Chip Hance and Ray Goldberg. "The NutraSweet Company: Technology to Tailor-Make Foods." Harvard Business School Case #N9–589–050, 1988.
7. Alfred D. Chandler, Jr. *Strategy & Structure*. Cambridge, Mass.: MIT Press, 1969, see generally.

   _____. *The Visible Hand*. Cambridge, Mass.: Belknap Press, 1977, see generally.
8. Schnaars. *Megamistakes*.
9. Upton Sinclair. *The Jungle*. Pasadena, Calif.: 1942.
10. Janice Castro. "Making It Better." *Time,* November 13, 1989, p. 79.
11. John P. Newport, Jr. "American Express: Service That Sells." *Fortune,* November 20, 1989, p. 80.
12. Hamid Noori, *Managing The Dynamics Of New Technology,* Englewood Cliffs, N.J.: Prentice Hall, 1990, p. 117.
13. Frederick Taylor. *The Principles of Scientific Management.* New York: Harper & Row, 1911.

    J. M. Juran and F. M. Gryna, Jr. *Quality Planning And Analysis,* 2nd. ed. New York: McGraw-Hill, 1980.

    W. E. Deming. "Quality, Productivity and Competitive Position." M. I. T. Center for Advanced Engineering Study, Cambridge, Mass., 1982.
14. Oliver Williamson. *Markets and Hierarchies*. New York: Free Press, 1975.

Bill Ouchi. *The M-form Society.* Reading, Mass.: Addison-Wesley Publishing, 1984.

15. Michael Porter. "From Competitive Advantage to Corporate Strategy." *Harvard Business Review,* May–June 1986, p. 43.
16. Joseph McCann and Roderick Gilkey. *Joining Forces.* Englewood Cliffs, N.J.: Prentice Hall, 1988.
17. David Halberstam. *The Reckoning.* New York: Morrow, 1986. Maryann Keller. *Rude Awakening.* New York: Morrow, 1989.
18. Schnaars. *Megamistakes.*
19. Cathy Coffman. "Tough Teflon Trivia." *Automotive Industries,* June 1988.

CHAPTER 2

1. See Searle Corporate Report: "Searle 1888–1985." Available from company.
2. "Searle 1888–1985."
3. Frederick Betz. *Managing Technology.* Englewood Cliffs, N.J.: Prentice-Hall, 1987, p. 222.
4. National Academy of Engineering and National Research Council, 1983. *The Competitive Status of the U.S. Pharmaceutical Industry, 1983.* Washington, D.C.: National Academy Press.
5. For additional background on the sweetener market, see generally, Chip Hance and Ray Goldberg. "The NutraSweet Company: Technology to Tailor-Make Foods." Harvard Business School Case #N9–589–050, 1988; Darral Clarke, "G. D. Searle & Co.: Equal Low-Calorie Sweetener." HBS Case #9–585–010; and Kim Lopdrup, "PepsiCo: The Aspartame Decision." HBS Case #9–55–078.
6. "Milestones in U.S. Food and Drug Law History." *An FDA Consumer Memo,* HHS Publication Number (FDA) 85–1063. William Grigg. "Part Two: The Making of a Milestone in Consumer Protection 1938–1988." *FDA Consumer,* November 1988. Wallace F. Janssen. "The Constitution and the Consumer: Discovering the Connections." *FDA Consumer,* September 1987; and "The U.S. Food and Drug Law: How It Came, How It Works." HHS Publication Number (FDA) 86–1054.
7. "A Primer on Food Additives," *FDA Consumer,* October 1988, p. 15.

CHAPTER 3

1. David Halberstam. *The Best and the Brightest.* New York: Random House, 1972.

2. Roy Rowan. "A Politician-Turned-Executive." *Fortune,* September 10, 1979, p. 88.
3. "NutraSweet—Health and Safety Concerns," report. Senate Committee on Labor and Human Resources, Washington, D.C., November 3, 1987.
4. "NutraSweet—Health and Safety Concerns," report.
5. Testimony of John E. Robson before the Subcommittee on Courts, Civil Liberties, and the Administration of Justice, on H.R. 1937: "Patent Term Restoration Act of 1981," November 18, 1981.

CHAPTER 4

1. Eben Shapiro. "NutraSweet's Bitter Fight." *The New York Times,* November 19, 1989, section F, page 4.
2. Wendy L. Wall. "Marketing NutraSweet in Leaner Times." *The Wall Street Journal,* May 7, 1987, p. 32.
3. Robert B. Shapiro. "Security Analyst Presentation". New York, N.Y., March 18, 1986. Copy available from the NutraSweet Company.
4. For a review of biotechnology concepts and applications, see Jeffrey Berg, "Developments in Biotechnology—And the Outlook for the Future." *Design News,* July 7, 1986; Gregory Daneke. "The Global Contest Over the Control of the Innovation Process: The Case of Biotech." *Columbia Journal of World Business,* Winter 1984; and Dekkers Davidson. "A Note on the Biotechnology Industry." Harvard Business School Case #9–384–214, 1984.
5. Gifford Pinchot III. *Intrapreneuring.* New York: Harper & Row, 1985.

CHAPTER 5

1. Roger Enrico and Jesse Kornbluth. *The Other Guy Blinked.* New York: Bantam Books, 1986, p. 74.
2. Michael Porter, Edward Hoff and Constance Irwin. "The Soft Drink Industry in 1986." Harvard Business School Case #9–389–196, 1989, p. 3.
3. "Diet Coke Kicks Off against Sugar Pepsi as 'The Move Is On to Diet Coke'." News Release, Coca-Cola USA, Atlanta, Ga., January 23, 1989, p. 3.
4. "Coca-Cola Products Consumed 200 Billion Times around the World in 1988." *The Coca-Cola Company Fact Sheet,* February 10,

1989; "Refreshing Facts about Coca-Cola," *Consumer Information Center,* Coca-Cola USA, Atlanta, Ga., June 1987.

5. News Release, Coca-Cola USA, January 23, 1989, p. 3.
6. Porter, Hoff and Irwin. "The Soft Drink Industry in 1986." Neil H. Snyder. "PepsiCo and the Cola War." McIntire School of Business, University of Virginia, 1986.
7. Snyder, "PepsiCo and the Cola War."
8. Chip Hance and Ray Goldberg. "The NutraSweet Company: Technology To Tailor-Make Foods." Harvard Business School Case #N9–589–050, 1988.
9. Eben Shapiro. "NutraSweet's Bitter Fight." *The New York Times,* November 19, 1989.
10. Kate Mahar. "Sweeteners: Quest For Stability Goes On." *Beverage Industry,* June 1987, p. 13.

CHAPTER 6

1. Michael Porter, *From Competitive Advantage.* New York: Free Press, 1985.
2. Tom Peters. *Thriving On Chaos.* New York: Perennial Library (Harper & Row), 1988.
Robert H. Waterman, Jr. *The Renewal Factor.* New York: Bantam Books, 1988.
3. Eben Shapiro. "NutraSweet's Bitter Fight." *The New York Times,* November 19, 1989.
4. Melissa Turner. "Prospects Are Dim for a Plant That's Sweeter Than Sugar." *The Atlanta Journal And Constitution,* August 14, 1989, p. A-5.
5. Warren E. Leary. "Thanks to Researchers, the List of Sugar Substitutes Grows Fatter." *Los Angeles Herald Examiner,* September 10, 1989, p. D-3.

Warren E. Leary. "Big Payoffs Are Pushing Research into More Sugar Substitutes." *Seattle Post-Intelligencer,* September 13, 1989, p. C-4.

Hal Straus. "The Search for Sweet Perfection." *The Atlanta Journal and Constitution,* February 6, 1990, p. D-9.

Donna Tapellini. "Competitors Are Beginning to Circle NutraSweet's Territory." *Adweek's Marketing Week,* December 5, 1988, p. 38.
6. Edmund L. Andrews. "Patents; New Sweeteners Developed by Coke." *The New York Times,* December 3, 1988.
7. Shapiro. "NutraSweet's Bitter Fight."
8. Shapiro. "NutraSweet's Bitter Fight."

9. Gordon Block. "Will Fake Fat Yield Plump Profits?" *Time,* May 25, 1987, p. 57.

   Gwendolyn Cates. "NutraSweet Sets Out for Fat-Substitute City." *Business Week,* February 15, 1988, p. 100.

   Calvin Sims. "NutraSweet Reports Fat Substitute." *The New York Times,* January 28, 1988, p. D-1.

   Wendy L. Wall. "Monsanto's NutraSweet Unit to Report It Has a Fat Substitute, Sources Say." *The Wall Street Journal,* January 19, 1988, p. 32.

   Wendy L. Wall. "NutraSweet's Fat Substitute, Seen Beating P&G to Market, Promises Diet Revolution." *The Wall Street Journal,* January 28, 1988, p. 25.

10. Alex Kotlowitz. "FDA Will Review Monsanto Unit's New Fat Substitute." *The Wall Street Journal,* February 1, 1988, p. 6.

   Joanne Lipman. "FDA Rules Pose Marketing Snag for Fat-Substitute Products." *The Wall Street Journal,* September 22, 1989, p. B-4.

   Wendy L. Wall. "FDA Urges NutraSweet Co. to Submit New Fat Substitute for Review by Agency." *The Wall Street Journal,* January 29, 1988, p. 2.

11. Julie Liesse Erickson. "NutraSweet May Develop Its Own Simplesse Brands." *Advertising Age,* February 8, 1988, p. 4.

12. Laurie Levy. "Even Dieters Deserve a Treat." *North Shore,* November 1989, p. 196.

   Judy Matthewson and Lenny Glynn. "Have It Your Way . . . Fast-Food Chains Get Health Conscious." *Longevity,* September 1989, p. 76.

   Bill Richards. "Will NutraSweet's Diet Cafe Be a Taste Of Sales to Come?" *The Wall Street Journal,* November 22, 1988, p. 87.

   David Snyder. "Lagging NutraSweet to Test Dessert Stores." *Chicago Business,* week of July 11–17, 1988, p. 1.

   Carolyn Walkup. "NutraSweet Open Dessert Cafe." *Restaurant News,* December 12, 1988, p. 23.

   See also: Advertisement, "Join the Deserve Team Today." *Chicago Tribune,* October 1, 1989, sect. 19, p. 5.

CHAPTER 7

1. James D. Watson. *The Double Helix.* New York: Atheneum Publishers, 1968.

2. Daniel Bell. *The Coming of Post-Industrial Society.* New York: Basic Books, 1973.

————. *The Cultural Contradictions of Capitalism.* New York: Basic Books, 1976.

3. Jacques Ellul. *The Technological Society.* New York: Vintage Books, 1964.

Lewis Mumford. Technics and Human Development: The Myth of the Machine. New York: Harcourt Brace Jovanovich, 1966.

4. Alvin Toffler. *Future Shock.* New York: Random House, 1970.

Alvin Toffler. *The Futurists.* New York: Random House, 1972.

See also, generally:

Kenneth Boulding. *The Meaning of the Twentieth Century: The Great Transition.* New York: Harper & Row, 1964.

P. F. Drucker. *The Age Of Discontinuity: Guidelines to Our Changing Society.* New York: Harper & Row, 1968.

R. B. Fuller. *Operating Manual For Spaceship Earth.* Carbondale, Ill.: Southern Illinois University Press, 1969.

Donald Schon. *Beyond The Stable State.* New York: Random House, 1971.

5. Henry Adams. The Degradation of the Democratic Dogma. New York: Macmillan, 1919.

6. Jeremy Rifkin. telephone conversation reported in the *Whole Earth Review.* Winter 1988.

7. Edward Wenk, Jr. *Tradeoffs: Imperatives of Choice in a High-Tech World.* Baltimore, Md.: Johns Hopkins University Press, 1986.

8. Richard Saul Wurman. *Information Anxiety.* New York: Doubleday, 1989, p. 3.

9. Bell. *The Cultural Contradictions of Capitalism.* p. 36.

10. Russel L. Ackoff. *Redesigning the Future.* New York: John Wiley & Sons, 1974.

11. Jeff Pfeffer. *The External Control of Organizations: A Resource Dependence Perspective.* New York: Harper & Row, 1978.

12. Michael E. Porter. *Competition in Global Industries.* Boston, Mass.: Harvard Business School Press, 1986, p. 315.

13. Michael E. Porter. *Competitive Advantage.* New York: Free Press, 1985.

Michael E. Porter. *Competitive Strategy.* New York: Free Press, 1980.

14. George Gilder. *Microcosm.* New York: Simon & Schuster, 1989.

15. Robert H. Waterman, Jr. The Renewal Factor: How the Best Get and Keep the Competitive Edge. New York: Bantam, 1987.

16. Otis Port. "A New Vision For The Factory." *Business Week,* Innovation 1989, p. 146.

17. Russell Mitchell. "Nurturing Those Ideas." *Business Week*, Innovation 1989, p. 106.
    Kiyoshi Suzaki. *The New Manufacturing Challenge*. New York: Free Press, 1987.
18. See as examples: Philip Kotler, Liam Fahey, and Somkid Jatusripitale. *The New Competition*. Englewood Cliffs, N.J.: Prentice-Hall, 1985.
    Kenichi Ohmae. *Triad Power*. New York: Free Press, 1985.
    Michael E. Porter. *Competition In Global Industries*.
19. Zachary Schiller. "An American Tragedy: How A Good Company Died." *Business Week*, April 17, 1989, p. 8.
20. Gene Koretz. "Business Talks a Better R&D Game Than It Plays." *Business Week*, August 21, 1989, p. 20.
21. Michael E. Porter. *Competitive Advantage*.

CHAPTER 8

1. Peter Drucker. *Innovation and Entrepreneurship*. New York: Harper & Row, 1985, p. 150.
2. Geoffrey Vickers. *Value Systems and Social Process*. Middlesex, England: Penguin Books, 1968.
3. Kenichi Ohmae. *The Mind Of The Strategist*. Middlesex, England: Penguin Books, 1983, p. 2.
4. Richard Daft. *Organization Theory and Design*. St. Paul, Minn.: West Publishing, 1983.
    Jay Galbraith and Daniel Nathanson. *Strategy Implementation: The Role of Structure and Process*. St. Paul, Minn.: West Publishing, 1978.
    Lawrence Hrebiniak and William Joyce. *Implementing Strategy*. New York: Macmillan, 1984.
5. See Walter Kiechel III. "A Hard Look At Executive Vision." *Fortune*, October 23, 1989, p. 207;
    William Lilley III. "Leadership: Beyond the Obvious." *Fortune*, October 9, 1989, p. 193.
6. Robert Miles, with Kim Cameron. *Coffin Nails and Corporate Strategy*. Englewood Cliffs, N.J.: Prentice-Hall, 1982.
7. Terrence Deal and Allan Kennedy, *Corporate Cultures*. Reading, Mass., Addison-Wesley Publishing, 1982. See also, endnote #12, below, for additional cites.
8. Noel Tichy and Ram Charan. "Speed, Simplicity, Self-Confidence: An Interview with Jack Welch." *Harvard Business Review*, September–October 1989, p. 112.

9. Mariann Jelinek and Claudia Schoonhoven. *The Innovation Marathon.* Cambridge, Mass., Basil Blackwell, 1990.
10. John Sculley, with John Byrne. *Odyssey.* New York: Harper & Row, 1987.
11. Mel Horwitch and C. K. Prahalad. "Managing Technological Innovation: Three Ideal Modes." *Sloan Management Review,* Winter 1976, vol. 17, no. 2.

    Charles O'Reilly. "Corporations, Culture, and Commitment: Motivation and Social Control in Organizations." *California Management Review,* Summer 1989, p. 9.
12. Peter Block. *The Empowered Manager: Positive Political Skills at Work.* San Francisco, Ca.: Jossey-Bass, 1987.

    Robert Burgelman and Leonard Sayles. *Inside Corporate Innovation.* New York: Free Press, 1986.

    Lucien Rhodes. "Corporate Antihero John Sculley." *Inc.* October 1987, p. 49.

    Edward Roberts. *Generating Technological Innovation.* New York: Oxford University Press, 1987.

    Thomas Stewart. "New Ways to Exercise Power." and "CEO's See Clout Shifting." *Fortune,* November 6, 1989, p. 52 and p. 66, respectively.
13. Richard Brandt, Jonathan Levine, and Robert Hof. "The Future of Silicon Valley." *Business Week,* February 5, 1990, p. 54.

    Lawrence Franko. "Global Corporate Competition: Who's Winning, Who's Losing, and the R&D Factor as One Reason Why." *Strategic Management Journal,* vol. 10, 1989, pp. 449–74.

    Gene Koretz. "Economic Trends." *Business Week,* February 5, 1990, p. 18.
14. Joseph Morone. "Strategic Use of Technology." *California Management Review,* Summer 1989, p. 96.

CHAPTER 9

1. Lois Therrien. "Foodmakers Will Taste Humble Pie." *Business Week,* January 8, 1990, p. 80.
2. Kathleen Deveny. "Lesson of the '80s: Emphasize Health, Eliminate Hassles." *The Wall Street Journal,* November 28, 1989, p. B1.

    Julie Erickson. "The Healthy Alternative." *Advertising Age,* November 13, 1989, p. 3.

    Fran Labell. "Biotechnology: 'Natural' Key to Unlocking Improved

Flavors And Foods." *Food Processing,* December 1988, p. 20.

Anthony Ramirez. "In Hot Pursuit of High-Tech Food." *Fortune* December 23, 1985, p. 85.

3. James Hirsch. "U.S. Diet Mixes Indulgence, Health." *The Wall Street Journal,* December 6, 1989, p. B-1.

4. Russell Mitchell. "Does This Cereal Belong in the Medicine Cabinet?" *Business Week,* July 24, 1989, p. 22.

5. Carole Sugarman and Richard Morin. "Poll Shows Shoppers' Skepticism about Nutrition Claims." *Chicago Sun Times,* January 25, 1990, p. 2.

6. Robert Cross. "Label Lingo." *Chicago Tribune,* October 5, 1989, sec. 7, p. 1.

Mitchell. "Does This Cereal Belong in the Medicine Cabinet?"

Therrien. "Foodmakers Will Taste Humble Pie."

7. Marion Franz. "Aspartame Does Not Cause Headaches." *Diabetes,* October 1989, p. 51.

8. Robert Johnson. "Nutritionists Detect a Dark Side in New World of Food Substitutes." *The Wall Street Journal,* February 3, 1988, sec. 2, p. 1.

Janny Scott. "The Promises And Perils Of Designer Foods." *Los Angeles Times,* October 8, 1989, magazine sec. 2, p. 57.

9. Laurie Freeman. "The Day When 'Fat' Won't Be Sinful." *Advertising Age,* November 13, 1989, p. 3.

10. Harold Edmondson and Steven Wheelwright. "Outstanding Manufacturing in the Coming Decade." *California Management Review,* Summer, 1989, p. 77.

11. Albert Link and Gregory Tassey. *Strategies For Technology-Based Competition.* Lexington, Mass.: Lexington Books, 1989.

Ira Magaziner and Robert Reich. *Minding America's Business.* New York: Random House, 1982.

Thomas McCraw. *America Versus Japan.* Cambridge, Mass.: Harvard Business School Press, 1988.

Bruce Scott and George Lodge. *U.S. Competitiveness in the World Economy.* Cambridge, Mass.: Harvard Business School Press, 1985

12. Associated Press. "Future 'Information Gap' Is Likely for Poor People, Report on Technology Says." *The Atlanta Journal and Constitution,* January 31, 1990, p. C-7.

13. Ronald Bailey. "Ministry Of Fear." *Forbes,* June 27, 1988, p. 138.

APPENDIX A

REGULATORY HISTORY AND APPROVAL SUMMARY

The NutraSweet Company

ASPARTAME
U.S. REGULATORY CHRONOLOGY

1973 Searle files petition for use of aspartame in a variety of food categories.

1974 FDA publishes regulation approving aspartame.

1974 Objections are raised by two individuals claiming aspartame causes mental retardation, brain lesions, and neuroendocrine disorders.

1974 FDA refuses to stay approval of regulation on safety grounds but grants hearing on all pending objections.

1975 FDA raises questions of uterine polyps in rats following administration of DKP (a breakdown product of aspartame). Hearing on objections deferred until issue resolved. Pathologists from the Armed Forces Institute of Pathology as well as other experts review data and find that DKP is not associated with uterine polyps. Objectors advised of findings and plans for hearing proceed.

1975 Based on "preliminary results" of an audit of certain animal studies, FDA stays approval of aspartame and the hearing until validity of data resolved.

1976 FDA recommends to Searle that independent outside third party validate data submitted by Searle from "critical" studies. Recommendation is discussed.

1977 Searle contracts with Universities Associated for Research and Education in Pathology (UAREP) to audit 12 studies. UAREP was recommended by FDA.

1978 Objectors raise issue that aspartame causes brain tumors in rats.

1978 UAREP report submitted. Conclusions of reports submitted by Searle found to have been supported by valid data.

1979 Objectors agree to Public Board of Inquiry (PBOI) to resolve objections instead of a formal administrative hearing. Objectors agree with FDA on issues to be addressed by PBOI.

1979 FDA affirms Searle data authentic and publishes announcement to convene PBOI to resolve objections.

1980 PBOI held to resolve objections relating to brain lesions, neuroendocrine disorders, mental retardation and brain tumors.

1980 Searle sues FDA to obtain a decision from the hearing process.

1980 PBOI issues decision — (1) Aspartame does not pose risk of mental retardation, neuroendocrine disorders, or brain lesions. (2) Data does not rule out possibility of aspartame associated with brain tumors in rats. Recommends another rat study be done at lower doses. Searle, Bureau of Foods and objectors file exception. Validity of data as an issue is raised by objectors in appeal.

1981 Commissioner upholds PBOI decision on mental retardation, neuroendocrine disorders and brain lesions. Commissioner reverses PBOI decision on the issue of brain tumors due to factual and statistical errors of interpretation by the PBOI. Commissioner also reviewed a new study in rats with no evidence of brain tumors.

1981 Aspartame approved by FDA; no appeal of decision made by objectors to Court of Appeals as provided by law.

1982 Searle submits petition seeking approval for aspartame use in carbonated beverages.

1983 FDA approves aspartame for use in carbonated beverages. Approval announcement specifically addresses each of the comments received during review process.

1983 Objections to approval for carbonated beverages filed raising all prior resolved objections.

1983 FDA refuses to grant stay.

1984 FDA refuses to grant another hearing as all issues previously addressed and resolved or the objection is based on mere allegations without scientific support.

1984 FDA approves use in multivitamins.

1984 Objectors file appeal in U.S. Court of Appeals to obtain a hearing.

1985 Court of Appeals upholds FDA Decision, based on a lack of "material objection to the safety of aspartame that would require the FDA to grant a hearing."

1986 Objectors file a writ of certiorari with the U.S. Supreme Court.

1986 U.S. Supreme Court refuses to hear the case.

1986 CNI petitions FDA to remove aspartame as imminent hazard.

1986 FDA approves four new categories of aspartame use (frozen novelties, teas, juice-based products and breath mints) and denies imminent hazard petition.

1986/ CNI objects to new regulations and appeals to U.S.
1987 Court of Appeals on FDA denial of imminent hazard.

1987 GAO issues final report declaring FDA acted properly in its approval of aspartame.

1987 NutraSweet submits petition seeking approval for aspartame use in baked goods and baking uses.

The NutraSweet Company

PRODUCT SAFETY

Aspartame has been shown to be safe for the general population including people with diabetes, pregnant and nursing women, and children. Individuals who need to control their phenylalanine intake (PKU patients) should treat aspartame like any other source of this common amino acid.

INDEPENDENT REVIEW

In addition to extensive review and monitoring by the U.S. Food and Drug Administration over more than 15 years, aspartame has been reviewed and found to be safe for the general population by:

- The Council on Scientific Affairs of the American Medical Association;

- The American Academy of Pediatrics;

- The American Diabetes Association;

- The Canadian Diabetes Association;

- The Epilepsy Institute;

- The Joint Expert Committee on Food Additives of the United Nations and World Health Organization;

- The United Kingdom Committee on Toxicology of Chemicals in Foods;

- The Scientific Committee for Food of the European Economic Communities;

- The Canadian Health Protection Branch; and

- Regulatory Authorities in 63 nations worldwide.

Aspartame is the only low-calorie sweetener allowed in foods and beverages in Canada.

APPENDIX B

NUTRASWEET MISSION STATEMENT

Our Mission Statement rests on the belief that we can choose our future.

Each sentence in the Mission Statement represents a choice about the kind of company we want to become. But what we actually become will be decided by the choices we make every day.

The Mission Statement will be as true and as real as we choose to make it.

If we treat the Mission Statement as a meaningless expression of empty corporate sentiment, then that is exactly what it is. But if we treat it as a practical guide to our conduct and the standard against which we honestly measure ourselves, then it will, over time, become an accurate description of our company and ourselves.

Please read the Mission Statement carefully and take some time to think about it. If it describes the kind of company you want to be part of, then I would ask you to help make us that kind of company. The way to do that, I believe, is for each of us to make a personal commitment to our Mission Statement, to adopt it as our own—and, above all, to bring it to life, in all our actions, every day.

I emphasized the words, "each of us," in the last sentence because we cannot succeed if some of us make that commitment and some do not. A personal commitment to the Mission Statement means not only that we will live by it, but that we will also expect the people we work with to live by it as well. There can be only one set of ground rules for our company, and the Mission Statement is it.

Bob Shapiro

184

OUR MISSION

Our Mission is to bring better food choices to consumers through the application of advanced technology. We will carry out our Mission by following five fundamental principles:

1. Consumers trust our products to be helpful and safe. We will keep faith with them in everything we do.
2. NutraSweet brand sweetener is the foundation of our business. We will support the brand so as to achieve its full potential and to maintain preeminence in the markets in which we compete.
3. We will find and develop new products that meet evolving consumer needs for nutrition, healthfulness, and enjoyment in foods and beverages. These products must provide financial returns that justify our investment in research and development.
4. We will maintain uncompromising standards of quality while constantly reducing costs.
5. We will form and maintain close working partnerships with our customers. We will listen carefully, keep their perspectives in mind, and strive to add value to their businesses and ours.

Beyond these principles, certain values must guide us in carrying out our Mission:

Integrity: We insist on honest and fair relationships among ourselves and with all the people who are affected by our actions: consumers; customers and suppliers; health and nutrition professionals; government agencies; and the citizens of the communities where we live and work.

Courage: Our history is one of courage and dedication in the face of difficult challenges. We must continue to have the courage to challenge the status quo and act on our beliefs.

Innovation: We will maintain an atmosphere that fosters creativity, innovation, and intelligent risk-taking. We will be open-minded, flexible, and driven by a sense of urgency. We will guard against rigidity and bureaucracy that stifle initiative.

Teamwork: Our Mission requires individuals with diverse talents and experience to work closely together to achieve shared goals. We prize individual achievement and, at the same time, we insist on cooperation, mutual support, and teamwork.

Commitment to Each Other: We will devote extraordinary care to the hiring and development of outstanding people. We will encourage personal growth and reward achievement. We will treat each other with dignity, evenhandedness, and respect. While our Mission commits us to change, we will work to minimize the disruptive effects of change upon lives and careers.

This statement of our Mission and the values that support it represent the cornerstone on which our future will be built. We will consult it frequently, reexamine it periodically, teach it to those who join us, and measure ourselves against it. We will give it real and practical meaning through our actions.

INDEX

A

A&W Brands, 85
Abbott Labs, 85
Acesulfame K, 108
Ackoff, Russell, 126
Acquisitions
  pace of, 136
  trends, 13–14
Adams, Henry, 120
Advertising; *see also* Marketing
  agency appointment, 56
  direct to consumers, 57–58, 78,
    100
  NutraSweet expenditures on, 3
  in soft drink industry, 80–81
Agricultural Department, 29
Ajinomoto Company, 15, 34–35, 47
  aspartame production in, 36
  as competitor of NutraSweet, 107
  European presence of, 105–6
  offer to purchase NutraSweet,
    92–93
  process technology used by, 7,
    60–62, 64–66, 165
  role in investigation of aspartame,
    16–17
  Searle's joint venture with, 35,
    65–66, 71, 158
Aldacticide, 37
Aldactone, 37
Alitame, 107–8
Apple Computer, 147
Applications Technology, 103
Artificial sweeteners
  advertising of, 58
  competition among, 107–8
  market for, 26–28

Aspartame
  approval of, 47, 48, 87–88,
    181–83
  competitors for, 107–11
  cost of, 3–5, 98
  critics of, 48–50
  early marketing efforts of, 32–36
  as exploited surprise, 17–18
  FDA investigation of, 36–38,
    43–47, 49–51
  low-cost production of, 97–100
  100 percent requirement, 88, 89
  patent for, 1, 15, 25, 34–35,
    51–53, 105, 165–66
  post-patent strategy for, 97–98
  pricing of, 86
  profit from, 1
  regulation of, 30, 181–83; *see also*
    Regulatory process
  as result of intentional innovation,
    8, 10
  sales in food companies using, 3
  shelf life of, 102, 104
  test marketing of, 47
Association of Official Analytical
  Chemists, 32
Augusta plant, 60, 68–76, 100
Australia, 106
Automobile industry, 14, 128
Azarnoff, Daniel, 42, 54

B

Baar, William, 87
Baby bust, 124
Bada, Jeffrey, 50